SACRED DANCES

The Gurdjieff Movements

Nella Denzey Markoe Liska

KARNAK PRESS

KARNAK PRESS

SACRED DANCES

THE GURDJIEFF MOVEMENTS

The author wishes to acknowledge Fiona Nicol and Robin Bloor for their assistance in editing this book.

First Edition: May 2023
ISBN: 978-1-957278-04-9
Printed in the United States of America

This book is dedicated to my beloved teachers, Jeanne de Salzmann, Jessmin Howarth, Alfred Etiévant and Paul Reynard.

May they all rest peacefully at the side of His Endlessness.

With the greatest love and appreciation for all they have given me.

Sacred Dances: The Gurdjieff Movements

Contents

Mr Gurdjieff

Foreword

The word "dance" usually suggests rhythmic movement that provides artistic expression and entertainment. Nothing could be further removed from Gurdjieff's Movements. They are sometimes called "Sacred Dances," but the adjective sacred is easily misunderstood outside its religious or spiritual context. The Movements are not a performance art; they might be thought of as contemplative or meditative musical Gymnastics if one has never seen or participated in them.

A Movements class depends on an instructor and a musician, usually a pianist, working closely together to lead the class collaboratively. These are the external resources; the essential part is interior for each participant.

Our thoughts, feelings and bodily movements are usually controlled by mechanical associations, but participation in Movements can provide opportunity for attentively aligned centers to guide consciousness

Jessmin Howarth taught Movements in Europe and

America from 1924 until her death in 1984. She explains:

> *"Most of us have found that through the Practice of Movements, one has direct experiences which lead the body and feelings to an understanding of the Work ideas which might, lacking this means, have remained simply a theory...*
>
> *And we discover in ourselves many hitherto unexpected possibilities. We find that one can collect one's attention, that one can be 'awake' at times and have an overall sensation of oneself; ...that Quietness of mind, an awareness of the body and an interest of feeling can be brought together and that this results in a more complete state of attentiveness in which the life force is freed and one is sensitive and open to higher influences. Thus, one has a taste of how life could be lived differently.*
>
> *Because that is so, the Movements are sacred for us, and we try to keep them as pure as when they were first given and protect them from distortion and superstition."*

Anyone currently undertaking the search for an opportunity to practice authentic Gurdjieff Movements exercises is going to find it a challenging quest; discrimination is necessary. Movements are not just a dance form. They are meant to be practiced as an essential part of Gurdjieff's teachings, which they communicate and support in definite ways. One is introduced to Movements classes only as part of being authentically engaged in his teaching.

Since Gurdjieff's death in 1949, many groups continue to meet that were initiated by him, his direct pupils, or by senior students of pupils who worked with Gurdjieff and were authorized to transmit his teaching.

With little or no publicity, these groups have, for decades, maintained their commitment to the study of Gurdjieff's teaching.

Jessmin Howarth's extensive and meticulous choreographic notes, the documentary films that Jeanne de Salzmann directed and the Movements classes offered by instructors who studied with Gurdjieff and/or His pupils maintain Gurdjieff's legacy.

However, as decades passed, an increasing number of individuals and organizations have borrowed and indiscriminately adapted from Gurdjieff's legacy for their own artistic or commercial purposes. Theatrical productions, public demonstrations, weekend workshops and private lessons, as well as films of musical calisthenics that imitate and emulate Gurdjieff, are increasingly available from individuals who – despite their claims to the contrary – have no connection to Gurdjieff's legacy.

J. Walter Driscoll.

2023

Sacred Dances: The Gurdjieff Movements

Introduction

I s the written word truly helpful for a discipline that is performed by the body? After long consideration and many thousands of Movements classes, I realized there was an enormous amount missing about this extraordinary art. Important material needed to be shared in order for the "Movements" to continue as Mr. Gurdjieff intended as part of his "Work."

As the Movements move more and more into the general population, "teachers," depending on where or by whom they have received the Movements, are often not given the guidelines and conditions under which to pass them on honorably and correctly. At this point in time, important conditions which may seem trivial need to be acknowledged. One needs to realize that this art form can only be transmitted in the manner it was intended by people who have been trained correctly.

Movements are much better understood by being executed in a class of serious students with a truly knowledgeable instructor. But there are very few of those left. Almost none. This book is intended to assist those who wish to pass on Mr. Gurdjieff's extraordinary material and who undertake a serious study of the Gurdjieff Movements as part of his complete System.

It is also about other aspects of the Gurdjieff Movements that are rarely or never spoken about.

Additionally, this book is intended as a tribute to those extraordinary people who brought Gurdjieff Movements to us; Alfred Etiévant, chosen by Mr. Gurdjieff to bring Movements to the world, and his wife Lise, Jessmin Howarth, whose Dalcroze students were in the first Movements classes, Marthe de Gaigneron thanks to whom we have her notes for the Movements done in Mr. Gurdjieff's time, Josee De Salzmann, an extraordinarily beautiful teacher, Pauline de Dompierre, whose wonderful mind enlivened the exercises and of course, Solange Claustres, who brought her extraordinary quality of moving as an example, to Mme. Jeanne de Salzmann herself for her continued work to carry forward the demanding and beautiful "inner work" in the Movements. Also of note are Natalie Etiévant – the extraordinary teacher of South America; Paul Reynard – who taught for 40 years in America; and his right-hand man – Andre Enard, the kind and wonderful.

These people devoted their lives to the continuation of this remarkable art form, and what they brought deserves to be taken care of with great respect. These wonderful human beings were my teachers in this extraordinary journey that is the Gurdjieff Movements.

Since this is a book about the Movements, we will go straight to that, and if you are interested in finding out a little about my remarkable introduction to the Movements, you can go to the epilogue at the end of this book.

Please note that if you are looking for actual positions and notes about specific Movements, you will not find them in this book. If that is the case, this book is not for you.

Sacred Dances: The Gurdjieff Movements

CHAPTER 1

Creation and Execution
Parts of a "System" for Everyday Life

According to Mme. de Salzmann, whom Mr. Gurdjieff left in charge of The Work or The Fourth Way, the beginning of the Movements occurred in a hotel room in Tiflis.

She told me that Mr. Gurdjieff asked her to stand inside an empty bed frame in the room.

He told her to raise her right leg, and then he left the room to make coffee. According to her, when she attempted to put her leg down, he said, "keep leg up." So she continued standing on one leg for quite a while. Then he said, "change leg," and she did. Those of you who have experienced it will recognize the beginnings of the *First Obligatory*.

Gurdjieff wanted the average person to understand the concept of "being" as it applies to their daily lives. He wanted us to experience a "change of state." We know that he studied medicine and the science of vibrations and that he was trying to find the most useful way to bring people to a deeper connection to what we understand as "sensation" as the quickest way to self-observation and a change of "state." From a meeting in 1922, he said:

> *"All centers should work simultaneously; great results can be obtained. Intellect (is) hampered by lack of physical movements, of which we have few, owing to the lack of use of limbs. More movements that we have, i.e., the greater the variety of physical work, dances, etc., the greater the possibility of getting new thoughts and 'seeing". Development of the moving center wakens the other two. Real Work from the body upwards must begin from it. Every feeling stopped helps self-remembering by that feeling. All energy spent on conscious work is an investment that spent mechanically is lost forever. Study movements and postures and through them (one) can easily read emotions and thoughts"* [1]

Gurdjieff wished to help people learn to remember themselves "Always and Everywhere" – in other words, in their daily life. This self-remembering is an integral part of the understanding required for a change of Being. In order to increase the ability of people to be present in themselves, he needed to find a way to correct the years of bad education and lopsidedness of humans.

---

[1] *Gurdjieff's Early Talks 1914 - 1931, p140*

A way in which all three centers could be involved properly, and the proper functioning of the body could be free to work in harmony without each center interfering with the others. When asked why he didn't start with psychology as Jung did or many other psychiatrists, he laughed and said that when everyone was collected around the "front door" (the head), he decided to go around the "back door" where there was nobody looking!

Participation in these extraordinary Movements makes it possible over time to maintain a sensation during the day as you go about your daily activities. This, in turn, allows the exercise of self-remembering to be possible.

Mr. Gurdjieff intended the Movements to be a part of his complete teaching. They are beautiful in themselves, but it is doing a major disservice to his Work to treat them only as exercises or dances. The Work consists of many parts – some for each center of the body, and it is a complete and well-thought-out system. Mr. Gurdjieff wrote three books:

"*Beelzebub's Tales to His Grandson*" (also known as "*All and Everything*"), "*Meetings With Remarkable Men*," and "*Life Is Real Only Then When I Am*." These books are accompanied by "*Views from the Real World*," which is a record of lectures, meetings and questions from his pupils and the recently published "*Paris Meetings 1943*."

Mr. Gurdjieff's ideas are also well documented by P.D. Ouspensky in *In Search of the Miraculous* and *The Fourth Way*. These books constitute the primary body of Work ideas, and studying them is one of the core practices of

The Work. These ideas are work for the brain.

The Movements (some of which have direct correlations to All and Everything) provide work for the

Thomas de Hartmann

body primarily, but also the mind and the emotions.

And the extraordinary music, some of which was composed by Mr. Gurdjieff himself, with the help of Mr. Thomas de Hartmann and Mme. de Salzmann (who improvised at the piano for the original Movements classes), provides beautiful fuel for the emotional center as

Making costumes from CS Nott's book, Journey of a Pupil

Mr. Gurdjieff working at scenery with Alexander de Salzmann in the background also from CS Nott's Journey of a Pupil

Photo of one of the sets, courtesy of Dushka Howarth.

well as a "call" to the body to move in time with the beat.

There is also Project work for the emotional center. This began as making costumes and stage sets for the original Movements demonstrations given by Mr. Gurdjieff. Notably the stage ballet *The Struggle of the Magicians* with scenery by Alexandre de Salzmann, who was a noted stage designer of his time.

Pupils who traveled with Mr. Gurdjieff also learned how to cook with him – and he was known to possess an extraordinary palette. According to Solange Claustres in her book *Becoming Conscious with G.I. Gurdjieff.*[2]

> *"G always did the cooking himself, often for over twenty people, with such dexterity, taste, refinement, and extraordinary knowledge of dishes from many countries, never making*

---

[2] *Becoming Conscious with Gurdjieff, p55*

anything in exactly the same way. To create this recipe on the spur of the moment, in his place, seemed to me simply impossible."

In recent years many types of projects have been undertaken in The Work, but the focus on theatre is still there today. Students were also taught to garden and build walls and buildings as part of their training toward being present.

So each component of this system; the Ideas, the Movements, the Music and the Work Days (which is what Project Days or Workshops are called today) provide a well-rounded and integrated possibility to actually observe oneself with the intention of growing one's Being, which can only come about through Self-Observation. Many people these days say that the Work is not a "system," meaning that it is not a program, but in my experience, this is demeaning the actual Work, which most certainly has all the components of a "system" and when followed definitely does give results which are quantifiable. It is the highest compliment to Mr. Gurdjieff to acknowledge the completeness of his understanding of us as "three-centered beings."

There is no other system or body of knowledge which touches every part of the human being, both physical and spiritual, as The Work does. This is why it is referred to as the "Fourth" Way.

Sacred Dances: The Gurdjieff Movements

CHAPTER 2

A Three Centered Approach

As part of the understanding of the Movements, we must acknowledge their structure right away, abiding by the Law of Three, which is a very important concept in the Work.

Three major components must be present to have a proper Movements class in which the pupils receive an impression of themselves.

There must be:

1) The class
2) The instructor
3) The musician

These three are equal, and the quality of their attention contributes to the outcome of the class and the impression received by everyone present.

1) The Class

MOST IMPORTANT: Movements are never done by one person alone. They are a group activity, and this group of people is representative of a microcosm of the universe. Dr. William Welsh expressed it well by saying that each person has a responsibility in the class, as each is "an independent part of an interdependent whole."

It represents what Mr. Gurdjieff called "Organic Life on Earth." As such, no one person is ever "featured" …ever.

It is important to understand the format of the class.

Classes should be a mixed arrangement of men and women in order to have the proper balance and tone quality throughout the class. Mr. Gurdjieff has Movements for mixed groups, others specifically for women and for men. Some groups mistakenly think that women should be on one side of the class and men on the other [as in "sittings"], but this dilutes the intention that Mr. G specifically placed in "mixed" Movements. At the same time, a men's "dervish" would be counterproductive to be executed by a class made up purely of women. There are wonderful classes for women only. Please leave the Men their own classes.

A class should be composed of 6, what are referred to as "files," counting from 1 to 6 from left to right as you look at the class from the front.

In general, there are two decisions about the placement of the pupils, which is a concession to height and the ability of everyone in the class to see the instructor and vice versa.

Taller people (usually men) are in File 1, and the shortest people (usually women) are on the far right in File 6.

File 1	File 2	File 3	File 4	File 5	File 6
(tallest)					(shortest)

There is also another configuration where the tallest people are in Files 1 and 6 and the shortest are in the center.

File 1	File 2	File 3	File 4	File 5	File 6
(tallest)		(shortest)	(shortest)		(tallest)

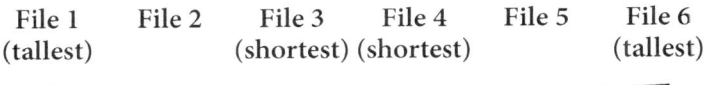

That being said, there is not really a hard and fast rule about this, except that the convention is that a man always needs to be in File 1 Row 1 (i.e., the left-hand corner). This is the "leader" of the class as far as the class motion is concerned, and that is why it needs to be a man (who represents the "active" principle in the Work). The responsibility of this person is the location of the class in the room. Everyone lines up with that person to his or her right, with the final say on the class location coming from File 1, Number 1. This is particularly important in multiplications, or other Movements with large displacements so that everyone in the class does not run into the walls or other objects in the room (like the piano).

This is one area where novice instructors fail to take notice. People in the class cannot have a good experience if their arm is touching the wall every time, or when they move forward, they are almost on top of the piano. It is the job of the instructor and also of the person in File 1

Row 1 to see that this does not happen. The rest of the class stands in rows directly behind the front row.

So when addressing the class, every person has a "location," i.e., 3rd File, 2nd Row. (see diagram below)

Files	1	2	3	4	5	6
Row 1	1.1	1.2	1.3	1.4	1.5	1.6
Row 2	2.1	2.2	2.3	2.4	2.5	2.6
Row 3	3.1	3.2	3.3	3.4	3.5	3.6

(for some movements there are 7 files)

This "location" has many interesting concepts in the study of Identification – a key concept of the Work.

For example, most people go to the same spot out of habit or a sense of security each week. Very few choose to actually change position. This is, of course, more work, and for anyone actively seeking to understand Movements in order to study them, it is a necessity to be for a time in every location in the class.

Then there is the tendency to feel attached to "my" spot. The position in the front row (which usually is taken by those who have a better facility in Movements) is a responsible one (because one has to think of those who are following behind you). It is also easier to see the Instructor without anyone else in the way, but this often has an ego attachment which can serve as good "inner work" for the pupil. What does the pupil want from the class experience? What in him/her do they want to serve? An instructor must be mindful of removing someone from the front row and replacing the pupil during an exercise, as this causes a reaction that must be recognized. It is inner work for the student, but the instructor must be sensitive to this.

By seeing his/her eagerness to be in the front row, the instructor can observe how serious the pupil is in his/her wish to work and, sometimes, how oblivious he or she is to their incapacity to do so and the "ego attachment" to being front and center. By moving people to the front row or, conversely, moving them to the back, there is a direct opportunity for the pupils to see their reactions. This can and should be done as a rotation so that sometimes Row 3 needs to be in front, and sometimes Row 2. This is particularly useful in Multiplications so that every person has the opportunity to move to the new position without seeing someone in front of him.

This takes away the tendency to copy and also gives the opportunity to sense the initiative and responsibility of the front row.

There is a challenge in each place in the class. Being at the back means blocking one's view of the people in front of you so one is able to do one's own work. But often, people choose the back rows because they can copy and rely on the work of those in front of them. One needs to examine this attitude; perhaps it's laziness, fear or lack of self-confidence. One needs to overcome fear and inner considering in order to experience the value of the Movements.

It is simply a good policy to rearrange files every so often so each person can experience a new perspective of the class and of the Movement and receive a new challenge, especially if the Movement starts to become habitual or mechanical.

Moving particular people in the class on an individual basis needs to be done with care and with love for the pupils involved. It should never be a "power play" on the part of the instructor or as "punishment." These types of things do not belong in The Work. The Work is never about manipulating others.

Classes are ideally three rows (that is 6 x 3=18 people). More than that makes it difficult to see from the fourth row back. Less than that makes it difficult to have an atmosphere of energy in the class. It is important to start a class with at least one row (6 people).

Most Movements require six people, although there are unison Movements and also Movements with seven people in the front row. There are also a few Movements with 5 Files and some with 4 Rows. For Multiplication Movements, there must be 6 Files.

In Gurdjieff's day, there was a beginner's exercise called "Copying," where one person stood in front of the class and took a position. Then after one count or two, the first row took the position, and then on the next count, the second row took the position while the first row took the new position that was shown from the front. Thus at any one time, each row was one, two, or three positions behind the person in front, forcing them to pay attention while simultaneously observing the one coming up. This is a very useful exercise and is good for classes to adopt today.

(Copying) 1939 demonstration courtesy of Dushka Howarth.

There were also frequent times when one pupil would be brought out in front of the class to demonstrate something done well for the benefit of those having trouble. This practice seems to have fallen by the wayside, and that is probably a good thing because the possibility of ego gratification of the pupil "selected" probably does more harm than good.

The issue of personal space is interesting to note here. The pupils need to be far enough apart so that they do not touch each other when moving. On the other hand, it is useful work studying when the pupils need to work very closely together so that their shoulders are almost touching. This allows each person to observe his/her own reactions to their personal space that they have in their daily life.

It is amusing to see how some of us never wish to be

very close to someone else and always leave too much space. And then, there are those who insist on pushing the person beside them (sometimes they are cognizant of this and sometimes not). Some people even try to "organize" the person beside them by "helping" them, telling them when and where they should move. There are so many fascinating opportunities to understand oneself in the class!

Some Movements require each row to "move as one," as in the *Tibetan Masques*. Some Movements are more fluid and require the immediate movement from one's place so that someone else can "step into my shoes," as it were. Movements such as *Les Vagues* offer this possibility, as well as some "marches." The acceleration of speed within a Movement is also a fascinating study and requires great attention to keep in harmony with everyone in the class.

2) The Instructor

In order to be a good Movements Instructor, you need to have had many, many years of classes yourself taken by competent knowledgeable instructors – not a pianist or a dancer who became enamored of Movements. Respect the extraordinary Movements material and don't "invent" or "improve" on something you don't understand. If you haven't learned Movements from an authorized Gurdjieff instructor, don't even try to pass anything along. This material is on many levels, and one needs a respect for this large understanding as well as an understanding of the human condition in oneself to be able to approach it.

Gurdjieff with Alfred Etiévant center, Lord Pentland left

It is a necessity to be able to Work on oneself in front of the class without your inner work being visible in addition to observing the inner work of the class. Also, to be able to be attentive to the form and structure of the entire class as well as the external positions of the students. And remember – it's not about you – you are in service to the class. You are privileged to be in this sacred space of the class and to see the exposed labors of people in the class as they struggle with the tasks at hand. Do not abuse this. This is a sacred trust. Do not take this on unless you understand that it is a service.

You are there to give energy to the class via your inner work and understanding – not take it! Not everyone who wishes to instruct the Movements is a suitable candidate.

Another requirement for instructing is a facility for

moving and a quick mind with an excellent grasp of Work ideas. And most important – a question about how to instruct better, how to "see" more about the energy and state of the class and individuals in it, and a humility about one's own capacity.

Needless to say, there are very few people with this combination. And every year, they are getting to be fewer and fewer as those with a direct link to Mr. Gurdjieff are no longer here.

Jessmin Howarth (above[3]) was instrumental in forming the first Movements class with Mr. Gurdjieff. She examined many people who aspired to be Movements Instructors in Gurdjieff Foundation groups and removed many people from the Movements' Instructors workshops if she felt they didn't have the appropriate qualities required for an instructor. Just because you want to be a Movements instructor doesn't mean you will be a good one. And at the present time, only those people trained by the Gurdjieff Foundations fulfill this require-ment at all, and even not all those people. Movements, however much one would wish it, should not be taught by those who did not receive proper instruction purely

---

[3] *Picture courtesy Fiona Denzey*

The picture above, courtesy of Dushka Howarth, shows Mr. Gurdjieff seated watching a Movements class. Beside him in order are Mme. Ouspensky, Mrs Nicoll and Maurice Nicoll. Behind the piano is Alexandre de Salzmann while Mr.de Hartmann is playing but only his ear is visible near to the pillar.

because so much of what can be received is omitted.

There are numerous people on the internet "teaching" Movements who are untrained and therefore are deceiving their students by calling their classes Gurdjieff Movements. If you wish to attend a Movements class, please make sure that the instructor is an accredited Movements instructor from the Gurdjieff Foundations, trained under the auspices of Mme. de Salzmann and Marthe de Gaigneron or their direct students. There are Gurdjieff Foundations in most of the large cities of the world.

It was thanks to Marthe Gaigneron that we have the Movements because she was instrumental in making notes of the Movements after each class with Mr. Gurdjieff. It is these notes that were compared with the recollections of the other members of the first row during Mr. Gurdjieff's instruction. These are the basis of the Movements that we work on today. It is direct material brought by Mr. Gurdjieff himself. The music for these classes was improvised by Mme. de Salzmann and later written down by Mr. de Hartmann.

These days there are many people who exploit the Movements as a new type of dance form and use this source for financial gain. Some people are so misinformed that they think Movements can be "enhanced" or used as the basis for a creative movement that they invent. This demonstrates a fundamental misunderstanding of what the Movements are.

There are many examples of this on the Internet. Some Movements are "performed" to recorded music with incorrect tempos, and some are even done to music composed for a different Movement. And these inventions are given spiritual-sounding names and are even called Movements. Mr. Gurdjieff's Movements have an enormous amount of knowledge encoded in them, and anyone who thinks they can "improve" on this by adding ideas from other sources would be wise to study more deeply Mr. Gurdjieff's complete system.

Work in Movements is esoteric work on oneself and is never to be a "performance." In the Gurdjieff Foundations, the Movements are never shown except to one another to share work and, on very rare occasions, to prepare for a "demonstration" as an additional demand on the pupils.

Mme. de Salzmann made several Movements films intending to keep as much of this material alive and to see if "presence" could be transmitted through the medium of film – to show "inner work" and the quality it manifests. Since some positions, arrangements and displacements were adapted or altered for the films, they cannot be taken as exact reference material.

It is also important to note that Movements in the films made by Mme. de Salzmann were often edited from the originals. There are several reasons for this. Primarily it is for the safety of the material, which should not be copied because some of it is not complete. Secondly, it was for dramatic effect since the aim of the films was to express both the extraordinariness and the unusual nature of the content.

These films are usually only shown to members of the Gurdjieff Foundation groups, who all contributed to the making of these films.

To this day, they are under strict supervision. There have been, unfortunately, however, several pirated attempts which have shown up on the Internet, and this could not be more unfortunate because these are esoteric exercises, not dance forms for entertainment. And in any case, badly pirated films don't show the full view of each Movement, making it even more dangerous to try and reproduce them directly from a film. Mr. Gurdjieff said that if his Movements are not done in the correct tempo and with the correct weight and quality, they can produce *exactly the opposite effect to what was intended.*

The Work formed the International Association of Gurdjieff Foundations (IAGF.org) to try and stop some of this piracy. Since Movements are only to be taught as part of group work, it is not necessary to copy the material from these films because, for bona fide instructors, material is available for those who have seriously committed to the continual study of Mr. Gurdjieff's system.

At this writing, the only authentic expression of the Gurdjieff Movements that can be seen by the public is the sequence at the end of the film "Meetings with Remarkable Men" directed by Peter Brook, and those are incomplete on purpose.

3) The Musician

Probably even more important than the instructor is the musician. Why? Because the tone that the musician plays on the piano penetrates directly into the students in the class and affects them even without their knowledge. While the instructor directs the class and bears the overall responsibility for the inner and outer work of the class, the musician has a great effect. A musician in a bad mood can ruin the class. One who is "asleep" at the piano will influence the class and ruin anything the instructor is trying to bring.

It is not enough to play the written music for a class. Many Movements and exercises do not have music written for them, and it is necessary for the musician to be able to improvise well; not only for these Movements but for the time when the class is learning a Movement and will be doing repeated actions over a long time. Constant repetition of the same music at this time results in a bored and inattentive class as well as removing the "specialness" of the music. It is necessary for the pianist to be able to watch the class at all times (not have his/her nose buried in the music) and at the same time bring a clear, attentive improvisational presence by watching the class and bringing that quality of the Movement being studied from the piano.

Playing for Movements' Classes requires a technically skilled pianist both in sight reading and improvisation, as well as an understanding of the role that the music plays for the class. This is a very difficult undertaking and requires dedication and much practice. The requirement for this means that the pianist needs to understand the inner work required on that bench and accepts it willingly as his/her own personal work. A certain freedom from self-criticism and worry has to appear so that the pianist can become one with the class. At this point, a new melody (which is not automatic) can appear.

Mrs. Annette Herter trained the musicians of the New York Foundation for many years until she died in 1970. Under her tutelage, wonderful musicians brought their knowledge and expertise to be "under fire" as they

Annette Herter, picture courtesy estate of Elsa Denzey

struggled to let go of their egotistical playing and find a more real, sensitive way of accompanying Movements.

Most notable of them was my mother, Elsa Denzey, Karel Backer, who accompanied the film class at the New York Foundation for 40 years with incredible sensitivity, Stafford Ordahl and Laurence Rosenthal. Each of these people took on the task to train and pass on their understanding to the next generation.

Many beautiful pieces of music were created for the core Movements. Since Mme. de Salzmann (who was an excellent pianist) improvised for these original exercises, many years later, these melodies were put into a form by Thomas De Hartmann and comprise the basis of the music that we use for certain Movements today. As time

Elsa Denzey, Karel Backer, and Larry Rosenthal

went on and more Movements were remembered and notated by the first row of Mr. Gurdjieff's original class with the participation of Mme. de Salzmann and Jessmin Howarth, new music was needed. The musicians who played for these "new" Movements stepped in to compose various suitable pieces of music that we now use.

These musicians: Yvette Grimaud, Alain Kremski, Eduard Michael, Mitchell Rudzinski, Stafford Ordahl, Elsa Denzey, Karel Backer and Laurence Rosenthal have all contributed to the music currently in use for the Movements. Much of this sheet music was exchanged from Group to Group as was needed and has now been compiled into a more useful book form by Charles Ketchum and William Garodnick. This music needs to be respected since it was approved by Mme. de Salzmann and has been "vetted" by many instructors over time.

It is not to be improvised on or edited, or otherwise disrespected. It embodies the inner work of many people.

But the written music must only serve as a guideline for the Movements' pianist. There is no substitute for presence at the piano and the constant observation of the class and oneself simultaneously. The participants in the class are more sensitive to the inner "state" of the pianist than to the sound of the notes themselves; thus the tone quality of the music emanating from the piano can help to bring the class to another state, which after all is the aim of Movements.

See "Instructions for Movements Pianists" on the opposite page.

To qualify as a pianist for the Gurdjieff movements' classes it is necessary to have knowledge of musical theory, enough piano technique to be able to keep a regular tempo, to provide a variety of touch and pedalling.

It is a great help and important to have learnt the movements oneself, or, at least to have watched classes and heard how others play. The written music should be practiced until it is memorized sufficiently for the pianist, when accompanying, to look at the pupils.

With regard to the improvisations needed, these should be kept as simple as possible, the basic beat and rhythm being more important than a melody.

One can study the bass of the written pieces, memorize the series of harmonies and use the chord structure to keep the time, only adding a melody when it becomes easy.

As a help it is useful to study the Greek modes. Some of the music for the Gurdjieff movements are written in these as for instance: "The Thirty Gestures".

The scale most often used by M. de hartmann was the harmonic minor. No dominant seventh chords were ever allowed.

The note above was written by Annette Herter in a letter sent to my mother.

CHAPTER 3

Clothing

We may as well start at the outer – the Movements "costume," as it has been called.

Originally in Mr. Gurdjieff's day, the Movements outfits were designed similarly to the wardrobe of the Orient. This usually comprised loose trousers, with a sort of tunic top. The men wore a shorter shirt and the women a longer tunic. Mr. Gurdjieff wanted the clothes to be "peasant-like" but for the women still to be beautiful. Below is a picture taken from Stanley Nott's book showing "working on costumes" and a picture from a full demonstration in 1939.

See the photo on the next page. Note the loose harem pants (even for the men) and the sashes. Also of note are the shoes and gold headbands.

The general Movements "outfit" has remained much the same till this day for special occasions such as demonstrations. The earliest ones in the '50s were made of pure silk. This was a heavy sort of silk which used to be

1939 Demonstration, picture courtesy of the author's collection

called "washing silk." The problem with silk is that silk is a biological substance and disintegrates when exposed to light. Thus these costumes were kept in a large chest with tissue paper in between pieces in the New York Foundation. I assume they did the same in Paris.

Everyone was required to purchase white ballet shoes (the flat-soled, front-pleated type), and the women had to purchase camisoles for modesty under the very thin white costumes. Today, the latest costumes are made of a synthetic material, which tries to emulate the original as much as possible. But these costumes are only for special occasions – not for everyday classes.

There was also made, at one time, a collection of men's "dervish "costumes patterned after the costumes of the Naqshbandi dervishes. These had the very wide "skirts" that opened when whirling, just like the Sufi Whirling dervishes. These men's costumes were made by various Groups during Work Days specifically for Mme. de

Salzmann's films. They also included a fez, a sash and boots. Costumes were sometimes reminiscent of various countries and were made for the 1968 film, which was the only one photographed in full color. The women were adorned with jewelry which accented the delicacy of the Women's dances.

Each costume was made specifically for each person.

Today's Movements attire worn in class is a little bit different. The idea of the attire was to make a costume that did not impede the motion of the body in any way. For example, if you have ever worn a pair of jeans, you will see that at certain places, the jeans press on particular spots on your body. This is distracting. If you have a belt, you, without noticing it, press your body against the belt in a very subtle way. This creates tension. The idea of the Movements outfit is to not have any of this superfluous tension while trying to come to a relaxed state.

Various groups have experimented with this idea creating a type of "pajama." Others have adopted the convention requested by Mrs. Howarth of white shirts or blouses and either black chino-type pants or mid-length skirts. Mrs. Howarth requested this because she said that it made the class uniformity easier to look at from the front, and of course, it emphasizes that no one is "special," which is a key idea of Movements. The idea is to see the Movement, not the contours of the body. And not to express your personality through your clothes.

There is an amusing comment told to me by Mrs. Howarth. She said that at Franklin Farms in Mendham,

New Jersey, Mme. Ouspensky always wanted the women to wear long black skirts. By long, I mean what we call today "ballet length." This is so that when you bend over, the person behind you in your file does not get a view of your underwear.

Mme. de Hartmann was also a stickler for this. Here is a picture of some women preparing for the 1951 demonstration at the Fashion Institute of Technology, where you can see the everyday Movements costumes.

Picture courtesy of the author's collection
From left to right: Lady Pentland, Mary Sinclair, Dede Dahlberg, Beatrice Sinclair, Sheila Bura, Sylvia March. Back Row: Frank Sinclair, Barbara Wheeler, Sophia March, Charlotte Phillips.

Other groups let people wear what they want, they don't have to adhere to white and black, but they need a loose top and pants that do not restrict movement. Over the years, certain restrictions have been implemented for practicality and respect; no shirts exposing the stomach when you raise your arms vertically, no shirts with logos, no tank tops, women to always wear supportive underwear, no jeans, no short skirts, no sleeveless tops, no tight stretch pants or yoga pants.

Whatever the case, the class members are requested to reserve their Movements outfit for class only and not wear it to and from the class or for other activities. The donning of this outfit is to be used as "preparation" for Inner Work and needs to be kept sacred for this. Alfred Etiévant told us that you "change" for Movements class. That means when you enter the school, you remove your clothing which symbolizes your outer life, and you "change" into an outfit that is reserved for work on your inner life. This is the actual beginning of the class, and the clothing brings with it associations of one's wish to work seriously. It is a very useful reminder.

Appropriate clothing, of course, applies to the instructor as well. For women assistants, no revealing or body hugging wear – much as one might wish to demonstrate positions – but Movements are not comparable to a dance class, and the instructor needs to set an example.

Shoes:

Very important. Movements cannot be done in either socks or bare feet. That is because there is a need for a certain amount of traction with the floor so one does not slip, and also, conversely, a lack of traction so that one's feet don't stick to the floor when doing gliding or marching Movements. The only shoes that work for this combination are flat leather-soled shoes.

It is not so important what the top looks like, and over the years, there have been many candidates. Probably the longest-lasting is the Capezio flat ballet shoe but without the supportive sole. It is important that the student is able to sense the foot flat on the floor. There are also various other companies that make a stretchy gymnastic shoe [slipper] that works well. Either white or black or brown. No hard-soled shoes or street shoes.

That being said, my first Movement teacher Alfred Etiévant always wore hard street shoes in front of the class. Perhaps in the 1960s, there wasn't much choice. He managed to teach very well in them especially demonstrating complex rhythms, but I wouldn't recommend this to anyone! And now no teacher would let you do this, not to mention the fact that it destroys floors.

The Sash:

In the original pictures, you can see the sashes that were tied around everyone's waist. Because the pictures are black and white, it's hard to know what color they were.

In the '50s and '60s the sash was worn in the following manner. In a row of 6, File 1 was Red, File 2 Orange, File 3 Yellow, File 4 Green, File 5 Blue and File 6 Purple. If there was a File 7 in a Movement, File 7 was Indigo. Sashes were *for demonstration only* and, in accordance with the study of the Law of Octaves, reflected the colors of the white ray. This was particularly interesting in Multiplications.

As you can imagine, there was quite a lot of amusement when people's sashes didn't fit as they gained weight.

The sashes were very long and wound twice around the waist, with the end threaded up and over to make a pleat at the waist and then hang down. Putting on these sashes was a ritual; to prepare before a demonstration.

The sashes must be made of fabric of sufficient weight that it doesn't "fly" up when you are turning and hit another participant or the wearer himself. And, of course, they absolutely must be primary colors. Sometimes it is necessary to search far and wide for the exact rainbow colors. Please note that this tradition has absolutely nothing to do with the current identification with the LGBTQ+ movement.

The Headbands:

Originally in Mr. Gurdjieff's day and until the early '60s, the participants (both men and women) wore a thin rope-like headband made of gold thread. These were sized individually for each person. I assumed that this was an "angelic" motif to denote the sacredness of the Movements, but no one that I spoke to ever mentioned anything about this. However, on one occasion, the New York Foundation was preparing a demonstration for the 13th celebration and Mme. de Salzmann was conducting the class. She asked to see the complete costume and approved the headbands. On another occasion, after viewing the Movements that were to be done, she said that we did not "deserve" them. So – no headbands.

Hair and Jewelry:

There was to be no jewelry during demonstrations, only plain wedding bands which needed to be disguised with a flesh-colored tape. This was partly to make sure that no one got injured if an article caught on something and partly to go against vanity. In the weekly classes, people can wear earrings and rings but no chains, bracelets or watches: nothing that can catch on anything, make noise or are a display of personality.

All hair, for both men and women, must be away from the face and tied so that during fast head movements, it doesn't whip around and strike one in the face or be distracting to the participant.

In summary, each part of the Movements "costume" was chosen with care and has meaning, and there is a reason for it. It is not regimented, nor is it cultish.

I have seen some attempts at replacing the originals on the Internet, and they do not have either the delicacy or beauty of the originals.

In the recent picture on the next page, you can see a working class with the white and black outfits.

Austin Class B 2015

Sacred Dances: The Gurdjieff Movements

CHAPTER 4

Positions and Exactness

Many people often ask me, "How important is it to do the positions of the Movement exactly?"

The answer is VERY, but with understanding.

Movements are an exact language and have been composed in as thorough a way as *Beelzebub's Tales to His Grandson* was written. This means that every position has been carefully planned and thought out and has a specific function and meaning.

One of the aims of the Movements is to provide "new" and "different" positions in order to bring the body out of its habitual postures and gestures. There are very few associative postures in Movements, and this is intentional.

Mr. Gurdjieff had an incredible understanding of the human mechanism, which we call the body and how it functions. In composing the Movements, he utilizes every single part of the body in one way or another. Over the years, I have found it astounding that nothing has been left out. Everything is thought of. Even the tongue, fingers, eyes and toes. Everything.

By analyzing this completeness carefully, one can start to see the understanding that goes with that. In *Meetings with Remarkable Men*, Mr. Gurdjieff gives a description of a moveable ivory figure that he encountered in a Tibetan monastery.

In front of this figure, several students were learning to take the shapes of the posed figure. This indicates right away the importance of the joints in movement. Most forms of exercise, i.e., running, swimming, tai chi, make use of the muscles to move the body. Movements do not. Other than certain medical practices, this form of exercise is unknown. Hence you will not burn fat doing Movements. But the upside is that the Movements will make you well. How does this happen? Mr. Gurdjieff called his Movements "medicine."

In freeing up the joints with relaxation and proper placement, one's energy begins to flow correctly. This is similar to acupuncture and Chinese medicine, which concentrates on the flow of what is called "chi."

In taking the positions of a new Movement, one is immediately confronted with several things:

The new position is unaccustomed and frequently uncomfortable, and there is the necessity of holding it for a long time. The earliest Movements were simple canons (rotating positions) like *French #30*. Each position is held for four counts before moving on to the next.

While entering into each position, one has the opportunity to take the position instantly and then relax into it with sensation while at the same time occupying the mind with the next position in the sequence. This is simultaneous work for the body and mind while providing associations that come from the various sensations via the muscles.

This Movement provides the participant with an opportunity to experience this specific emotion intended when he or she is sufficiently observant. For example, being on one's knees with one's arms up is a "prayer-like" association. The position allows for a sensation in the chest that touches the emotional center. *It is important not to "label" internally the inner observations that one receives during Movements.* A completely free look at whatever presents itself via the position will show the pupil a remarkable vision of not only themselves but much more.

Then there is the fact that my body is not used to moving from joints, but only muscles. In ordinary life and activities, we "teach" our muscles to work harder. For example, at the gym, we build up muscles. This has no place in Movements. In relaxing the body and relaxing the joints, the energy that is natural to the body can be unlocked to flow more since we are all convinced that we are relaxed when there is actually a much deeper relaxation required. We need to better understand tension and relaxation in order to experience it fully.

The vast majority of people have very immature or untrained moving centers and take the positions that are shown in a very awkward way. Work on this can be aided by occasionally having the students either "correct" each other's positions or by occasionally using the mirror. This should not be used too often, however, because the goal is to do this from one's sensation of oneself, and this takes years. Everyone has individual body "quirks." It is these "quirks" that are directly related to one's picture of oneself, and nothing will change about this until it is seen in oneself. This is directly related to each person's "work in life."

When attempting to correct the pupils' positions, one must remember that this is a very delicate task and requires much skill and understanding. Some people react very badly to being "corrected," even to the extent that they leave the class. Does this say something about the size of the pupil's ego, or is it a reaction to some very harsh and insensitive corrections being given?

Correction can only be done with love and with the best intent for the person being corrected. You will bring the same thing to the attention of a pupil many, many times in the hopes that one day they will see it. (For example – not straightening one's arms when they are vertical. They will swear that their arms are straight (when you can see that, obviously, they are not). So, keep in mind that most people have very little sensation of their own bodies. That's why they are in Movements class. This sensation has to be deepened, and this can only be done by inner relaxation, which has to be learned over time. Miraculously this does happen, and often, the person who once had a problem ceases to have it anymore. But this is not from correction. It is from *their own understanding* derived from their inner work related to the other aspects of the teaching. As I said, all quirks are related to my picture of myself – this can only change by inner "seeing."

So, returning to exactness. Does it matter? Yes. And there are different forms of exactness required in the Movements. One of these is taking a position exactly as shown.

If the pupil executes a position poorly, for example, a bent elbow when it should be straight, you can see that this would impede the flow of energy to the end of the hand. This is a direct inhibition and, therefore, a desecration of the Movement. One could do these Movements endlessly with slightly distorted positions, and one will receive nothing since the Movement will have been reduced to the level of ordinary exercise. Could one get some benefit from this? Well, yes, but not the wonderful benefit that Movements were designed for.

Nearly all Movements have to do with a relation to the spine. This is obvious right away in *The First Obligatory*, in which Mr. Gurdjieff makes the admonition, "Must have back!". We are taught right away to sense our backbone and rely on it to move from.

This is possible if I "pull myself up" out of the hips and find the center of gravity, which is just around the navel. Once I find this point, it is possible to stay very firmly on one leg, using the back from which to "radiate" the arms and feet. In every Movement there is this "radiation" in which the arms and sometimes the legs are cantilevered out from the spine.

The head needs to be balanced perfectly on top of the spine with no forward motion, which is noticeable from stress and habit, particularly from using a computer and looking at the television. Nearly everyone these days has this strain. The head is very slightly pushed forward from the spine.

In the Movement *Tibetan Masques*, we have the spinal column moving forward at a very slow speed, with the head moving in the same way as the back providing a seamless unit from the toes to the top of the head.

Another form of exactness is in the way a Movement is executed. Every Movement has a "postural component." By this, I mean one in which the legs are straight underneath the hips, slightly apart, and the motion of the Movement is from one leg to the other with the knees soft and never "locked." This is seen in many Dervish Movements and some Prayers, for example, *November 22nd, November 12th* and intermèdes in *The Prayer for Instruction*. The movement, in this case, is with the weight shifting from side to side. This movement from side to side produces a flow of energy up from the soles of the feet all the way through to the head and gives the participant opportunity to experience his or her whole body as one connected sensation. If this basic movement is done with knees too bent, the whole energy flow upward is cut off at the knees. Unfortunately, internally there is not the correct flow of energy. And this is just one of the many "styles" of function in the Movements.

Another very important aspect of correctness is walking. We all assume that we can walk just "very well." Through a long study of Movements, we can see that not only is this not true, but everyone walks with certain aspects of their character front and central. Some walk on the sides of their feet; some are too heavy on the ball of the foot, some too heavy on the heels, some with inflexible knees and hips etc., etc. You have only to look at the vast array of shoe inserts made by Dr. Scholls to confirm that this is true. We do not walk guided by the very things that connect us with the ground but move forward with our heads slightly forward of the body, pulling ourselves along behind it. Our sensation of our feet on the ground, for most people, most of the time is not noticed at all. This "bend" of the spinal column from the neck forward is symptomatic of our lack of three-centeredness because it shows that we are being "run" by the head or by "habit," not even real thought. It is an indication that the energy that is being stored in the body is not reaching the head through the spine. Cut off; we continue to be immersed in dreams where we think we are "present." At the piano or the computer, the same thing can be observed. Body hunched at the shoulders, neck forward, spine bent as we identify with the task in our waking "sleep."

There are motions in Movements that we call "knee bends" or a "down, up" action where the body bends only at the knees, so the knees come forward and then return towards the body until standing straight. This simple motion can be done in many different ways, which are *all* important. In the knee bend down and up, providing the back is straight, there is a pumping action that is pulmonary in nature. My breathing is affected by the large muscles of the thighs. If this is absent or not done properly, the whole Movement loses its effectiveness.

There is yet another reason to watch for exactness. Each Movement of Mr. Gurdjieff's has a "message," if you want to call it that. Every Movement has a purpose. These are all different. Inaccuracy in the positions distorts this. In some ways, this is tragic; in others just comical. One can look on the Internet to see all sorts of these distortions. It is necessary to really understand the "point" of each Movement and also the fundamental principle behind a Movement if one has the confidence to "teach" the Movements. Unfortunately, many of these "teachers" are unaware of the other levels of these phenomenal creations and see them only as choreographies they can imitate or alter to suit their performance needs. Many look for a more "balletic" approach. That is to say, a "softer" position of the body.

Someone once asked Mr. Gurdjieff why his positions were, in their view, hard and stiff. He said, "Is more honest."

It is important to point out that Mr. Gurdjieff did not want people to make notes about his classes after they learned the Movements he gave them. It is only recently that I understood why he said this. Now, with the compilation of numerous "notes" and "official notes" that are around, people have begun to do three terrible things:

1) Teach Movements from those "notes."

   This is naïve. Movements are an oral tradition and need to be passed from teacher to student and so on. There are certain things in Movements that can never be "notated" properly, and so the person who learns like this is making an educated guess or, worse, a personal interpretation. This is not how to learn Movements. Particularly not noted is the nuance of a rhythm and the correct tempo of each Movement. You cannot guess this or sense it on your own. Tempo is an organic quality dependent on many factors.

2) People have begun debates over positions.

   One set of notes says one thing – another something else about the same Movement. Movements were given slightly differently at different times in their history – even by Mr. Gurdjieff. What is important is to remember that each position must be understood before one can make changes. It is best to transmit a Movement the way it was given and studied in a class and to remain "open" toward another "version" while studying each without being identified with a particular version.

   Thus, a set of notes may have been done at different times or just observed differently by the authors of those notes. Maybe neither of them understood the motion or was able to correctly describe it, let alone understand its meaning.

Remember that people make mistakes while note-taking. Often these discrepancies develop into an argument about who is *right*. But it is clear that the only way to understand Movements is by understanding the purpose behind each Movement – and there are very few instructors at the current time who understand enough about each Movement to make a judgment about which version or position is "correct."

For argument's sake, let us suppose that a manuscript is found in Mr. Gurdjieff's handwriting that notated a specific sequence of positions, but the paper had a hole in it where the 4th position should be. The question then arises, would we know what the missing position is? If we cannot accurately replace that position, then we simply do not know enough to make any kind of changes to the material as we have received it.

3) The Movements are a living teaching. That means that they are *in the moment*.

You learn what you are being taught at the time and work with that. Mr. Gurdjieff himself changed some Movements. What was appropriate for one time, or for a specific person, was not the same at another time. This does not mean you can make mistakes or change the Movement. You do not have Mr. Gurdjieff's knowledge. So you do what you have been taught, only transmitting what is deeply understood in your body and try to see yourself in this as well as possible to understand the difference in the positions or *from where* the objection comes within yourself. The Movements are for self-observation.

So, to sum up... yes, every Movement must be performed as correctly as possible without invention. And without compromising the motion or gesture. If one cannot execute a Movement in its entirety with accurate representation of positions, it is best not to work with that Movement and instead choose one which best suits one's abilities.

Sacred Dances: The Gurdjieff Movements

CHAPTER 5

Tempo and Rhythm

W hat is the very first sound that we hear as babies? Yes, the beating of our mother's heart. Every organ of the body has a speed or tempo of its own. Take the speed of thought versus the throbbing of an injury to the muscles.

Gurdjieff Movements have fundamental tempo and rhythm as their basis. Mr. Gurdjieff had observed East Indian dancing, where rhythms are done with the feet and the hopping dance movements of the Tibetan Lamas, as well as the flamenco rhythms of Spain and the uniform cadence of the Whirling Dervishes. He grew up in a country with beautiful folk dances and songs.

Gurdjieff Movements are not in any way a copy of any of these dance forms. Although Mr. Gurdjieff did encounter many folk dances, especially in Tibet, none of the Movements are copied from these forms. All Movements composed by Mr. Gurdjieff are authentically his because they work in a different way and merely utilize some of the outer ideas of some of those dances. One step here or there might be the same or a rhythm, but overall the completeness of the Movements is light years above the simple peasant dances that he saw. Part of the genius of Mr. Gurdjieff was that he was a man on a different level, and what he was able to understand was more complete than our knowledge.

In Movements, all body parts have a rhythm. This can be seen in the *First Obligatory*. There we see a speed that corresponds to the three parts of each center – the feet (Moving), the arms (Emotional) and the head (Thinking). We are talking about the mechanism of movement here, not the speed of the center. For example, the legs are slower because there is a larger muscle mass to move. The arms are lighter and, therefore, can move faster, and the head, when viewed as a muscle, can move the fastest. This exercise is also the introduction to using the head as a "limb" rather than a repository for thought. This is fundamental in Movements. For an interesting experiment, I was taught to try a rhythm with the feet and then try it with the arms instead. The difference in weight and speed between these two becomes quite obvious. Then try a rhythm of the arms and then do it with the feet.

In working on a specific Movement in a class, instructors have been led to think that one must always start with the feet because they are generally the basis of the Movement. This is misleading. Sometimes the class is not in that place inside to begin with the feet. They might be in a particular state when they enter the room, where it is more appropriate to begin with the arms of a Movement or even the head.

This is particularly important when the class is very scattered. Some Movements are easier to understand when begun from the arms since sometimes it is the arms that give away the structure of the Movement. A good case in point of this is *French #35* or the *Grand Ensemble*.

Tempo:

The speed of the Movement directly corresponds to the inner place that the Movement is trying to reach. This has a great deal to do with the center it touches. A Movement that is given with too slow a tempo will only impact the thinking center (the slowest of the centers). This will result in an incorrect perception of the Movement permanently.

A Movement that is given too fast will not be understood and experienced properly and will have to be repeated.

Each class is composed of a variety of people differing in life experiences, ages, as well as physical and intellectual capabilities and the correct tempo for the class to *learn* a Movement is necessary for the instructor to discover. This is difficult to assess because people are of differing temperaments, and this also changes with the number of years pupils have studied. However, the neuroplasticity of the brain is similar in its ability to comprehend, so it is possible, with an open mind, to see what is possible. Therefore, three aspects must be taken into account right away. There is the tempo of the class in their ability to learn, the ideal tempo of the Movement, which has to be known organically in the body of the instructor and the inner "being energy level" of the class. The instructor must be able to balance all these things instinctively.

The class will probably not be able to come to the ideal tempo of the Movement, which is new to them at first, but the initial impression must not be too far from it because their first impression will be retained in them forever. The instructor needs to determine the energetic level of their inner presence and bring it as close to the ideal tempo as is possible for them as they learn. And there is an ideal tempo for each Movement which cannot be arrived at by guesswork. It needs to be passed along from a qualified instructor and needs to correspond to one's under-standing. *Never let the music notation dictate the tempo.* The majority of the written music has only a suggested time signature, which is there only as a guideline and not gospel.

If this can't be done, it is better to show the positions of the Movement without any tempo or music and then add that after the class has settled into the positions. A good example of this is the Movement called *Eleven Counts.* Then after the class has all the positions, it can be brought up to speed. This is where the *Third Obligatory* is helpful. Here we see an example of speed and tempo. One can also note here that very fast tempi make the class break down in laughter or just give up. An understanding of this reaction is a vital part of the instructing and should be studied in the *Third Obligatory* exercise and in the Movement called *Three Canons*. How would it be possible to "keep my attention" when the stress level gets higher and higher? Very useful for life!

There is a caveat to this observation. Many new instructors think that speeding up the tempo of the Movement they are giving to the class will bring more "energy." This "energy" needs to be provided by the instructor and whipping the class to go faster or slower is a gross misuse of power. It just demonstrates what little understanding the instructor has.

Outside of these intentional exercises in tempo, doing a Movement too fast will kill the ability of the class to do it well and eliminate any chance for sensation of the body so necessary for inner work.

So how can I find the ideal tempo for the class? First, I must know what the ideal tempo for the Movement is from hearing or seeing it when I learned it. This is where I will find how to give it to the class — not relying on the pianist to "give" me the tempo. The instructor *must* have the tempo in his or her body when he/she steps in front of the class. If you don't – don't give the Movement.

When the tempo is completely understood, the class should be able to continue without the piano and maintain the tempo. This produces a class working together, which is a wonderful sound. It is useful when working with a specific Movement, for the piano to stop playing altogether as an exercise for the class to keep its own tempo. Also, for the pianist, under the supervision of the instructor, to deliberately speed up or slow down slightly to see if the class can keep in time with the tempo. This exercise increases the ability of the class to stay together intentionally.

Many people are both rhythmically and tempo challenged. This can be worked on with inner work on relaxation in their Groups and Workdays. I firmly believe that everyone has an innate sense of tempo (maybe not rhythm), but this has been covered over by fear and poor education. Being criticized in youth often results in people not trusting themselves and, therefore, not being able to "let go" enough to sense this tempo. It is particularly important that in the class, the students, particularly those challenged in this department, are not intimidated in any way. The instructor should never ever point out their inability but instead gently and with compassion encourage them to trust the class and the general energy of the class to carry them. In this way, the class energy can enable them to do what they cannot do alone. I have seen many people come to a new discovery about themselves this way.

Rhythm:

This is innate in some people, but some are not so lucky. The sense of rhythm comes from the connections between the centers, which in many people, have been severed through no fault of their own. Again, a nurturing atmosphere can do a great deal to help with this.

I cannot emphasize enough how important rhythm is to the study of oneself and Movements.

Many years ago, we did all sorts of rhythm exercises when I was learning from Alfred Etiévant. One rhythm plus another, plus another, plus another – all different. Each of these rhythms had to be repeated back – in order!

There are still some Movements to this day that are like that; for example, the *Multiplication of October 8th* and *American #7*. These are great attention exercises, but for the majority of today's students, it is an exercise in frustration. This is partly because there is little or no exposure to ethnic dances in America and some parts of Europe also. Among some ethnic groups, like Ukrainians, Irish, Greek, East Indians and Native Americans, dancing is still taught to children and continues through to adulthood. Rhythm is in their culture. Among North Americans, we have the 4/4 time signature, which is rampant in all "pop" culture here.

Often musicians who start to play for Movements classes are stymied by the plethora of different rhythms.

A particular musical knowledge of modes, key signatures and note values is necessary.

This sometimes presents too much of a challenge for some pianists. And many try insidiously to change the rhythms to ones that they understand. The instructor must feel the rhythm so well that it cannot be shaken from your body. That way, the musician can rely on you for help. Not everything is a "march" tempo. If the musician cannot play the rhythm requested, use a drum or show the rhythm yourself with your feet. This is fundamental to the understanding of Movements.

In Movements, there are rhythms in divisions of 4, 5, 6, 7, 9 and 12. This refers to rhythmic phrases – not musical counting. We have "rhythms" which carry a whole phrase (like the *Canon to 5*). This is executed along the entire row, with each person moving on one note of the rhythm. This way of expressing a "rhythm" is a more engaging way to learn and brings attention. Try a rhythm that the class knows, like Ravel's Bolero. They will laugh when they get it. There are several Movements that have a simple rhythm in which the accent changes, first on the first note, then on the second note and then on the last note.

The best use of rhythm is when the whole class is involved and feels the rhythm together. The best Movement for this is the *"Breast Beating" Dervish* or *Reading from a Sacred Book*. Here we have the entire class beating a pulse while moving together as a whole. It is a powerful force and involves each person in the class, making them part of an organic whole, which exemplifies Mr. Gurdjieff's saying of "organic life on earth."

Rhythms in 5 or 7 are not in our Western consciousness, so they are very useful for taking us into another place in ourselves. We have *Dervish #7* with a count of 2/4 time in the rhythm but 10 in structure or *Dance #5* with a waltz tempo of 3/4 but a count of – yes, you guessed it – 5. We in our Western culture are fixated on even timing.

Mr. Gurdjieff wanted to make use of other types of unknown rhythms, so there is a group of Movements that make use of the Morse Code. Knowing the dot-dash sequence of the morse intended, one does a complete Movement in this "rhythm."

To make matters even more difficult, we have Movements with different actions in the feet and arms. Usually, one of these is just a tempo against a rhythm. This makes it more possible to execute. For example, *French #5* is sometimes referred to as *The "Pointing Dervish."* Here we have a tempo versus a rhythm in the feet. Or the beautiful *Balancier*.

The best thing one can do to study rhythm is to focus on movements of the feet and legs. Learn the different qualities that are exhibited by the feet – i.e., stamping, marching, gliding, sliding, tip-toeing, and many others.

Mr. Gurdjieff even had some "games" doing this, which I have given to my classes. Learn to feel your feet and rely on them to express a rhythm and tempo. This is a foundation on which to build a sensation of the body.

Sacred Dances: The Gurdjieff Movements

CHAPTER 6

Balance, the spine and the brain.

F or this chapter, we will begin at the beginning, The First Obligatory. This note is from Mrs. Howarth, who was there with Mr. Gurdjieff at the beginning.

"One woman, a teacher of Philosophy was always begging Mr. Gurdjieff for information so that she could write a book about him. And Mr. G. said: "How can you understand me enough to write about me until you have learnt at least to do THE FIRST OBLIGATORY!"

Following (on the next page) are Mrs. Howarth's typed notes on this very important Movement which begins the series called "The Obligatories" in the Gurdjieff lexicon.

Jessmin Howarth
226 East 70th, Apt. 3E
New York, N. Y. 10021

FIRST OBLIGATORIES

History

As far as we know, the First Obligatories were originally dictated by Mr. Gurdjieff to Mme de Salzmann's Eurythmics pupils in Tiflis around 1916.

They were included in demonstration programs given in Tiflis, Constantinople, Paris, London, and America - until 1924. The evening always began with them. Everyone who came to the Prieuré was required to learn them. *(even first time visitors)*

In the early years watchers found them not only surprising but rather shocking, because unlike most dance movements of that period - Delsarte, Dalcroze, Isadora Duncan - they included no continuous or flowing (legato) movements; but each exercise was built up of a sequence of stops.

Someone once asked Mr. Gurdjieff about this staccato way of executing the movements. The answer was: "Is more honest." I have taken this to mean that in these movements one must move intentionally to a predetermined attitude, hitting it exactly with no shift or adjustment; so, each "stop" gives one an instant to be aware.

At the Prieuré, and in demonstrations *(to open the program)* the First Obligatories were always done in the following order:

1 - First Obligatory - arms; legs; head; and arms and legs together.

2 - First March.

3 - Counting - with "stops".

4 - Note Values.

5 - March Forward.

6 - Mazurka - twice through.

(Rosemary Nott also records them in this order.)

The First Obligatory is so clear in its intent and illustrates so many of the core principles of the Work. Mr. Gurdjieff realized the connection between balance and the brain well before it had come to light in medical science.

The plan of the First Obligatory is much like the Leonard DaVinci picture of [Vitruvian] man, from Wikipedia.

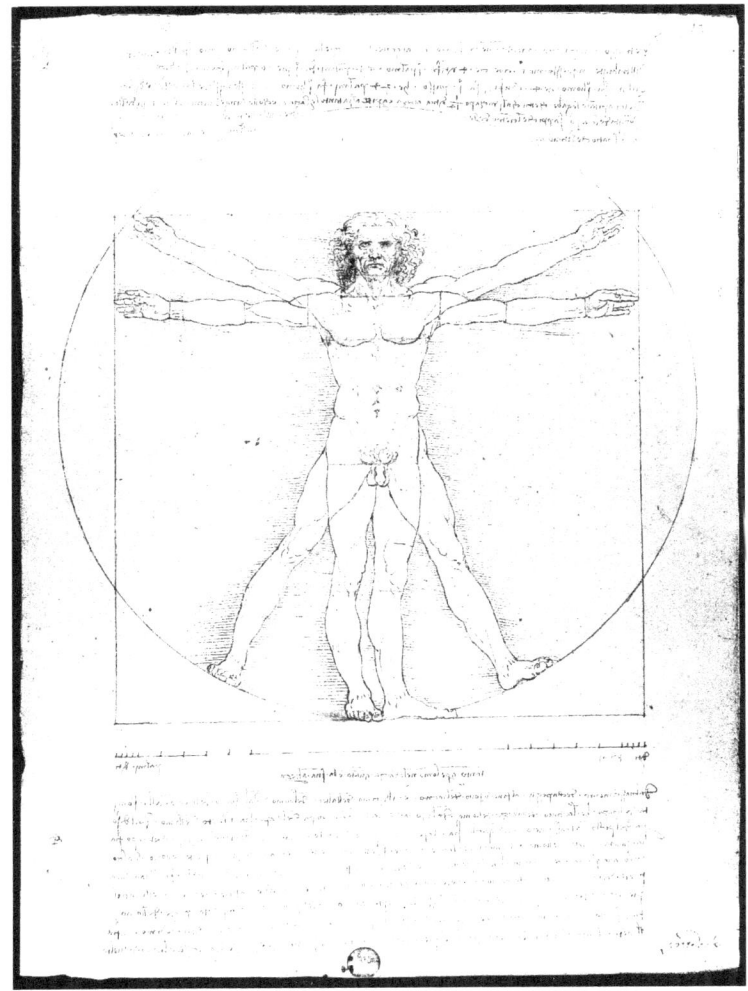

Here we see the limbs radiating out from the spine, which is the axis of the body.

So too, in the *First Obligatory*, we are advised by Mrs. Howarth to "pull the body upward while standing – out of your hips" to straighten the spine before we even begin.

This alignment allows the shoulders and pelvic girdle to hang straight down properly as opposed to the poor spinal alignment exhibited by most people upon standing. In the following diagram from Wikipedia, we can see the most common spinal positions.

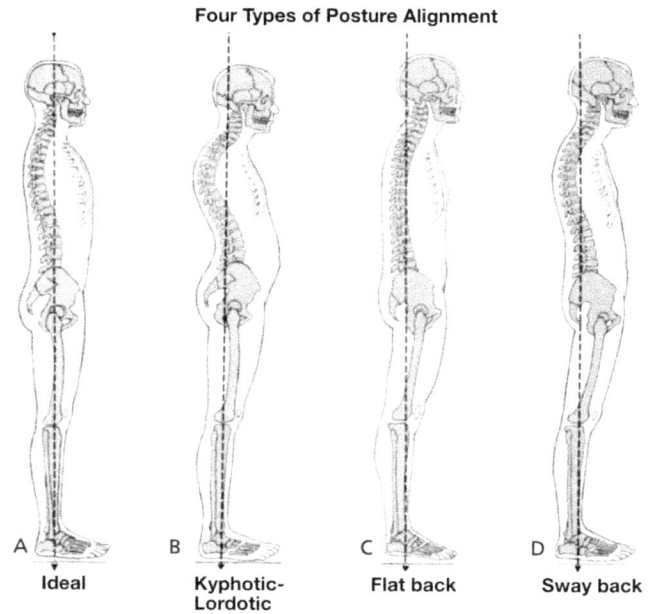

Four Types of Posture Alignment

A — Ideal B — Kyphotic-Lordotic C — Flat back D — Sway back

The posture marked IDEAL above is the posture to

begin *The First Obligatory*. In the Movement, we begin the first of three tempi with the arm movements. These are exact and radiate out in each plane from the spine. Nothing is left out – even up and down. At the same time, one needs to study the exact placing of the position and arrive on time, every time, even in the quicker and quickest tempo. The same degree of tension must be maintained in all three tempi as the natural inclination is to become inexact with the tempo change. This effort is the correct way of bringing your attention and sensation to the Movement.

It is interesting that the tempo begins slowly and then speeds up. The slower tempo gives the head brain time to place and execute the positions well, but then moves internally into the place where one must trust the body to find the same location again without interference from the mind. At the fast tempo, there is a disconnect between the head brain and the moving center, which allows the "brain" of the moving center to do its work properly. This is a wonderful illustration of the Three Centered Being – explained very well in *Views From The Real World* by Mr. Gurdjieff, in which each center: intellectual, moving and emotional, has three parts.[4]

Then we add the leg movements. This is definitely the most difficult part of the Movement. Why do we not start with this? Because Mr. Gurdjieff has laid out the pattern for the Movement in the most easily understood way possible. It also provides a clue to the importance of the

---

[4] *Views From The Real World. Page 155-158.*

Emotional Center.

In maintaining the balance by "pulled up out of the hips," we are called to find the center of gravity of the body. And once found, one strives to maintain it, keeping the hips and upper body still as the leg movements change. Correctly done in all three tempi, if watching the Movement from the front of the class, a person watching should almost see that there are no legs holding up this body, but it is as if suspended in space below the knees.

All changes in positions of the legs should be taken as if one is "replacing" the other – no jerk, no hop but a definite exchange.

Finally, the head is added, and this is a study in itself. In Gurdjieff Movements, the head is another limb. It is not the center of my personality, and it does not follow the eyes. The head movements are executed from the muscle at the back of the head, and the eyes remain static, as does the face. There is no change of expression. This takes most students a great deal of time to come to this sensation. In the way we live today, our head often leads the body, whether it is while walking or in any other occupation. This must disappear to do the Movements properly. The connection with the head must be internal, not external.

It is with the head movements that the question of balance is truly tested. At this moment, there needs to be an internal trust or letting go that the body can rely on its center of gravity, which by now has been established, and one can balance without looking but instead can rely on that muscle at the back of the neck to move the head in different directions.

Finally, there are the three parts: arms, feet, and head done together.

Doing the three parts together, in fact, takes the emphasis away from what doing them separately does. In doing them separately, attempting to keep the same quality and tone in each of three tempi, we have an effort in each center, which points out the relationship of each part to the center of gravity of the body. It also allows for the study of the relativity of speed in each body part and its center. One also notes the special aspects of the Movement, becoming very aware of the direction and plane of movement in relation to the spine. There is much of this to come in later Movements.

When doing all three parts of the Movement simultaneously, the relativity is lost in the effort of the body to coordinate the parts. This is another effort entirely, which comes from a different place in oneself. In an effort to "hold it all together," the focus changes to keeping the quality and tension the same in all three speeds as well as executing the Movement correctly.

After the *First Obligatory*, there are many other Movements that involve movements that radiate out from the spine. Notably among them are *The Grand Ensemble*, *Number 21*, *Old 21*, *L'Octave*, and the *Balancier*, but this is only a few. Each one of the above Movements has other principles encoded in them as well, as with many of the Gurdjieff Movements, and each one requires a finer and finer degree of sensation, which takes many years to realize. Some lovely Movements that have spinal sensation requirements are Multiplications, in which the body as a whole provides a framework for positions of the arms and head while at the same time moving forward and backward in space in the pattern of the Enneagram.

And as if to help with this poorly sensed part of the body – the spine – there are Movements in which bending is an integral part, such as *French #12*, where one bends to the side from the waist and then recovers slowly. Also, the *Cannon to 12* where there is a soft bending to each side. Mr. Gurdjieff uses each part of the body in a way which increases our sensation of it. In *Multiplication #41*, Mr. Gurdjieff cleverly incorporated all the yoga spinal positions. Here is bending down to the floor, twist right, twist left, bend back, straight up, and straight forward. Great workout!

Then there is direction of the body in respect to the room – 1/4 turns, 1/8 turns, 1/2 turns, and complete 360-degree turns.

Movements with these aspects, such as *Greek Letters, Two Rhythms, American #33*, and *June 15th*, are wonderful illustrations of the importance of keeping one's spine straight and body in alignment when facing another direction.

In facing a new direction in the room, we are faced with our inability to leave the previous one behind and take the new "front" completely. It is a great inner exercise to observe this tendency. How can I bring my complete presence to a brand-new direction, both externally and internally, into my life? In my life, can I be present to a new place, or do I drag the old behind me?

The spine provides a pivot point for turning (whirling), especially when one's arms are raised, such as in many of the Multiplications. Balance is provided by the counterbalance of the arms.

There are many Movements with turning – slowly, with intensity, and quiet turning. In the *Prayer in 4 Parts*, we have three of the four sections which have turning – all different. Then there is the movement *Multiplication with Turn on 5* and other multiplications where the 360-degree turn (in one count) is on the third count of the sequence. Some multiplications have all their displacements while turning, and many have the turns during a rhythm. For all these turns, an erect spine is absolutely obligatory in performing a flawless turn.

In studying turning, I have noticed over the years the differing effects of the brain. Aside from the obvious inner ear/balance correlation, there appears also to be a slowing down of the rotational axis of the body with age.

Turning with others becomes more difficult, perhaps because of the inability to drop one's own tempo, which becomes more acute with age. It is interesting to note, in conjunction with this, that older people are much more prone to falling, particularly with getting up and down and with quick movements.

Sacred Dances: The Gurdjieff Movements

CHAPTER 7

Sensation

A very large part of the Gurdjieff Work is about "sensation." This is distinguished by Mr. Gurdjieff as being different from emotions. For example, where heat is felt in the body as sensation. When we are happy or sad – that is emotion. In our usual language, we use these terms interchangeably. For example, one might say, "It feels hot today." But in the Work, Mr. Gurdjieff uses exact language for exact things.

I have heard it said, "There is a sensation exercise for every Movement." I am not sure where this remark came from, but I have never heard that ever, neither from Mme. De Salzmann or Mrs. Howarth or any other of Mr. Gurdjieff's esteemed pupils.

I think it is important to explore this topic because it is at the heart of the Movements' experience.

Sensation in the Gurdjieff Work is typified by an exercise in which the participant sits very still and directs his/her attention at first to the right arm, then the right leg, then the left leg and then the left arm. Each time this is done, there is an attempt to penetrate and sense more deeply the cells of the body, thus "coating" them with Presence. This is a very important exercise and is about encountering the reality of the body and the force that flows within it. This is life and Presence, and the practice of this exercise daily makes the ability to touch one's reality more and more readily available.

Because this exercise needs to be done in stillness, this is not the same as the inner exercises in Movements. Most people take years to be able to have a deep sensation of their bodies and are certainly not capable of doing this in Movements for a very long time. It is possible eventually, but Mr. Gurdjieff provided another answer.

Every movement is crafted to direct one's sensation to one part of the body or another. Sometimes several places at once. This type of sensation is inescapable. A few examples…

The Cannon to 12

Here we have a Movement that provides a very deep sensation of the thighs due to the knee bends and the feet rhythms. Do this Movement for a short while; you will have a sensation in your thighs. This is also true for *The Four Aums.*

French 21/American 22

This beautiful Movement calls for sensation in the arms and upper torso that continues for a very long time. This is not something you have to "do." It is there. It appears simply by executing the Movement.

French 14/American 25 "Breast Beating" Dervish

Here sensation vibrates in the feet. The alternating toe and heel with the rhythmic structure make it impossible not to have a sensation in your feet.

Tibetan Masques

Do this Movement for 5 minutes. After a limited time of working on this Movement, you will notice the sensation of muscles in your shoulders and back.

Forming Twos

In this exercise, there is sensation in the face with smiling face in one set of gestures and frowning face in the other.

Little Tibetan

There is a tongue movement on the third count of each set.

There are also finger sensations in the *Temple Dance* and toes in *Arche Difficile. Les Cercles*, done seated, has eye movements. These are heavily used parts of the body which we normally sense very little. There is sensation in your arms when doing the *Les Cercles*, with each arm going at a different tempo.

These sensations are calling you to be present in a very simple, clear way. They do not need any "exercise of sensation" added to them.

But, there *are* a few Movements which have specific

inner sensation exercises.

One of these is *Lord Have Mercy (French 11/American 18)* which has the actual Work circular exercise encoded in it. Another is the very beautiful *French 39/American 46 "meditation."* In this exercise, Mr. Gurdjieff points out very clearly the difference between sensation and feeling and visualization. This is a direct indication of how to work in Movements and also in life.

In some very advanced Movements, inner exercises of sensation can be added as additional work for the pupils. One such case is *The Initiates.* Another is the *"Stop" French 19/American 1*, which, although it is usually considered a beginner exercise, is not at all.

In considering this subject, for good instruction, it is necessary to observe the demands of each Movement that is being given to the class to see exactly what the demand is and if it is at an appropriate level for the class. Movements beginners should not be given Movements with any sort of "added" sensation exercise. Those encoded by Mr. Gurdjieff are better and clearer. Forming Twos is a perfect example. This not-so-simple dervish Movement has always been given to beginners. This Movement has a complicated rhythmic displacement, head and arm movements, words, and facial gestures. This is a lot for anyone, never mind someone new to Movements.

Why do the *Obligatories* not have "sensation exercises"? Because they are complete in themselves.

For example, the *First Obligatory* calls you to have a

sensation of the uprightness of your back and each part of the body is given attention in turn. This goes with Mr. Gurdjieff's comment for this Movement, "Must Have Back."

In the *Second Obligatory*, we are called to notice the atmosphere around the body and to understand the force necessary to keep up a certain tempo with differing qualities. Mr. Gurdjieff said, "Must Go Out."

In the *Counting*, no one can deny that one doesn't sense the body. It is used to measure space.

In the *March Forward* with raised arms at the beginning, we sense the body taking up a larger area of the surroundings (the body filling space), and that sensation culminates in the large body positions at the end, each of which not only evokes definite sensations but also some feelings.

In *Note Values*, the sensation comes from the back and its relationship to the arms all the way through the Movement. The shoulders, arms and then legs are highlighted.

And finally, the *Mazurka*, when done for more than 5 minutes, gives you a very clear sensation of the weight of your own body.

These are all sensations encoded in the Movements by Mr. Gurdjieff. There is never any need to "add" anything to Movements. As Mr. Gurdjieff himself said when asked why his Movements did not have more flowery gestures, "Is more honest."

I recently saw *Tibetan Masques* done by someone from a current group, and a "slap" on the thigh had been added, as well as a "foot stamping" gesture. These sorts of things right away tell you that this was not put in by Mr. Gurdjieff. There is no slapping in *any* Movement. Mr. Gurdjieff wants you to experience the internal stop that comes when you take a position firmly.

By adding a slap, you take that sensation away. This sort of thing has been added over time by overly enthusiastic instructors who get carried away. The Movements *do not need* any embellishment. If you want to emphasize something in a Movement, be careful not to exaggerate it and ruin the original intention. This is a very common problem among instructors. If you are going to separate out a part of the Movement to make it easier to learn, be absolutely sure you don't "add" anything in the process.

As far as "foot stamping" goes, there are Movements with foot stamping, like *French 20/American 31 – The "Treading" or "Tramping" Dervish* and *Old 39*. Foot "stamping" is a more automatic (hence less inner) action to do with the body, and adding it where it doesn't belong brings the Movement to an ordinary level. When it is placed in the above Movements, the weight of the body is directed downward on purpose and is difficult to sustain.

To add stamping to any Movement where the accent is forward, like *Tibetan Masques*, is not to understand the focus of the Movement.

Stamping in itself is uncommon in Movements because it is a movement of the body that originates in the knees, and nearly all Movements have weight exchanges that come from the pelvic girdle and the base of the spine. This is much more powerful than stamping and harder to accomplish but brings a presence in the body.

As the participants work at Movements over time, the ability to have better and better deeper sensation of oneself comes about. In the work of the most advanced classes, you can see the result of this fine sensation. The participants are quiet, present, and very sensitive. The gestures are controlled but not tight, and the flow of energy is liberal. This sensation can carry over into life and help enormously with everyday Presence.

CHAPTER 8

Breathing and words, vibration and sound

People have often thought that Movements do not have anything to do with the breathing exercises that are given in advanced stages of the Work. This is not at all true.

Mr. Gurdjieff did not want people to do breathing exercises because, as he advised, the taking over of the autonomic motor system by the *intentional* pulmonary exercise of the lungs interferes with the body's basic mechanism and can cause real damage in the future of the person trying these exercises. In consequence, we were never allowed to do breathing exercises of any kind until the addition by Lord Pentland, who brought some very minor breathing exercises in his sittings. Later this was expanded upon by Mme. de Salzmann, but only in certain rarified conditions. It was never done on any regular basis, and pupils were regularly warned: "not to try this at home."

Since breathing exercises are such an integral part of yoga and many other Eastern disciplines, it is worth examining Mr. Gurdjieff's actual practical work. There are three basic ways that the breathing participates in Movements: direct pulmonary actions, words, and floor patterns.

Direct Pulmonary Actions

Every Movement has either a pulse or a rhythm. Notice that there are no Movements with "erratic" pulses or "none at all." In the case of the pulse (many prayers and marches have a pulse), there is the direct action on the breathing to align it with the pulse by maintaining a beat. There is the individual struggle to feel the first (or only) beat of the rhythm and stay with it. There is an ongoing inner struggle to adjust one's tempo to correspond to the pulse, which is possibly quite far from each individual's natural zone, and when this is reached, there is a relaxing effect that takes place, regardless of the tempo. It is possible for an individual to breathe with a quite fast pulse due to this attempt to adhere to the beat and still be remarkably relaxed. A study of the acceleration of a pulse and the body's attempt to relax is apparent in *The Third Obligatory Exercise – Counting.*

The most common exercise where we can see the pulmonary action of movements is during "marching." This structured, regular beat is very close to the heartbeat tempo and can be utilized for a long period of time as a structure for inner observation since it is very natural. Movements have marches of all different types, from the

"First March" – *The Second Obligatory Exercise* to the very difficult *Tibetan Masques*. In the *First March*, we have a struggle to maintain the evenness of the actions despite very different gestures and qualities. In *Tibetan Masques*, we can see the involvement of the arms and shoulders – the upper parts of the torso – to add to the even beats of the tempo. The up and down movements of each arm emphasize the pulmonary functions of the lungs. There are many more examples of this in Movements, such as the *Balancier, Thirty Counts, Old 21*, etc. The necessity of maintaining a continuous motion in one arm and then transferring the motion to the other arm also contributes to even breathing in the lungs.

There can be a subsequent state change brought about with pulmonary action when everyone in the class is absolutely together. The oxygen in the room changes, and a finer substance begins to appear. This is a direct result of the evenness of the pulse being experienced by everyone together. Then with the addition of the movements of the upper torso adding to the effect, such as in *French 21/ American 22*, we have a Prayer.

A good example of this pulse in the whole class can be seen in *The Grand Ensemble*, one of the oldest exercises, but very useful for a class to study how to move together. Here the arm movements are all reinforcing the relaxation by each time returning to the chest in a regular in-and-out way that reinforces the breathing. The class as a whole has a "breath" cycle because it is divided into two halves, and with the bending, there is an "in" and "out" effect, which mimics the action of the lungs.

One of the most interesting Movements in this regard is *Polyrhythms*. Here there is an attempt to completely regulate several different pulses with the end result; if done correctly, is hypnotic for some people. The Movement definitely produces a change of state.

Words

This subject surrounds a broad set of things in Movements – from *"Ha,"* breathing out on each rhythm to *"wish," "effort," "be"* of *Forming Twos*.

In the case of the *"Ha, Ha, Ha"* or *Thrice Holy Lion* dervish Movement, the breath is just exaggerated to be expelled with force but not changed from what is actually going on in the lungs. This idea is in several "dervish" Movements, but not all. It is very strong in *"Ho-Ya Novices,"* accompanying the gestures of the arms, but not spoken at all in the *"Breast Beating" Dervish*, where the foot rhythms and the chest "beating" provides the "breath." Notice this Movement also requires the class to separate down the center, with each side moving away from the other, opening out and expanding like a pair of lungs and then going back towards the center.

Another sort of repetitive sound is the repetition of the word "Om," which occurs in some Movements, such as the *Four Oms* or the *Seated Circles "Om, Om, Om."* In the Om Movements, the work is to structure the mouth to make the correct sound in addition to maintaining the exhaled breath in a specific tone.

Listening to one's own sound is also required in some of them, such as *Om, Um, Am, and Im.* Here we have true breath work. The "world sound," as Mr. Gurdjieff puts it in *Beelzebub's Tales to His Grandson: All and Everything,* is a series of vowels that roll from the front to the back of the mouth, which is exemplified in the English vowels 'a,' 'e,' 'i,' 'o,' 'u' and sometimes 'y.' This is a sensation of the mouth which can be seen in Mr. Gurdjieff's "script" designed by Alexandre de Salzmann, that appeared on the study house walls at the Prieuré in Fontainebleau, France.

On another note, we have the "I" "Am" Movements, of which there are many. This specific word

was brought by Mr. Gurdjieff as an "as if" exercise. In other words, when one says the words "I"

"Am" one immediately realizes that one *is not* and, in this realization, a true wish and the observation of reality comes about. In this theory, by saying what one wishes and acknowledging the truth simultaneously, a change begins to take place slowly towards the aim of being present to the point that one day one can truly say, "I Am," and it will be true.[5]

This is true of all the "I Am" and "I Wish to Be" Movements. When one enunciates these words, there is also a corresponding sensation in the solar plexus or emotional center, which begins to bring about a change of state. These exercises of words should not be done without a qualified instructor who understands the significance of the actions and is able to take this

[5] *Views From the Real World, p239-241*

seriously. If a class says these words by rote, they will be spoiled and, therefore, of no value for the participant.

A good example of this is seen in *French 11/American 18 "Lord Have Mercy,"* one of the most beautiful of Mr. Gurdjieff's prayers. Here we see that the word corresponds to the sensation of the arm or leg and is appropriate to the pulse or tempo of that sensation. It is important that the words fall on the right place inside and are not just said "anyhow." All words in all Movements need to be said all together, with everyone using the same "pitch" of voice and with intention. This is usually neglected in Movements classes because many people do not know about this. For example: in *French # 5/American #2* (aka *the "Pointing" Dervish*), one note is to be held by everyone all the time as a sort of "drone" This is very difficult and changes the breathing in this vigorous Movement completely. There are no words in this Movement.

In the very beautiful *French #2/American #3, the Prayer in 4 Parts*, we have "Lord Help Me" in the second section, which again needs to be said with a sensation in the solar plexus and with gravity.

On the further spectrum of words, we have Movements like *"Lundi, Mardi"* and *Forming Twos*.

Forming Twos has a set of words which are alternately amusing and serious as a memory game while corresponding to the rhythm. The Movement also has facial gestures.

Singing

Last but not by any means least are Movements with singing. Here we have *La Gamme*, in which students sing the scale up and down. Also, the very beautiful *Do Mi Sol* – illustrative of the Law of Three – and the beautiful and touching *Hallelujah*. A whole year needs to be given to each of these Movements for the study of how the breath (and the note) leaves the body in a relaxed way. Everyone needs to have the same tone and same pitch. I don't think there is anything so beautiful as a whole class singing a triad in a quiet state. This is both touching and healthy for the body.

Floor Patterns

There are several Movements which are indications of the lungs, not only in the gestures but also in the patterns that the feet make on the floor. Most notable among these are *The Balancier*, *"Breast Beating" Dervish*, *Dance Number 5*, and *Lord Have Mercy*. Notice how in these Movements, the rest of the gestures complement the floor plan.

Vibration and Sound

Of course, the basic understanding of the Work, as brought by Mr. Gurdjieff, is the study of increasing the vibration rate of presence to create a type of "coating" for the second body. This is an actual physical process and everything in the Movements room must align properly to make this possible. This is the heart of the Work. This is what makes the difference between just doing gestures and actual "Sacred Dances." Without this understanding of Inner Work, the practice of Movements is lowered to the scale of regular dance.

Preparation is necessary to be able to access the possibilities on this level. First, one must be able to recognize the sensation of presence in oneself and be honest enough to sense exactly where I am on the scale of what I wish for.

Your daily work is critical here. This is the only starting point. One needs to be able to take a measure of the class's combined presence and be able to "tune" it to a higher frequency using the tools Mr. Gurdjieff has provided.

Take stock of the room, temperature, quality of the attention of the class, quality of presence in oneself, quality of presence of the pianist and volume and quality of the sound produced. Recognize what is not there. If any one of these things is absent, nothing higher will result. Be honest. Try to see the class's inner state. You will be able to do this by trying to "see" using the "double arrow" exercise talked about by Mr. Ouspensky in *In Search of the Miraculous*. Practice this often – even not in front of the class.[6]

Do not allow a poor state to emanate from the piano especially. This is delicate. You need to give the pianist room to work, but if the vibration coming from the piano is very coarse, ask him/her to stop and do the Movement without the piano for a while. Of course, that means you have to provide something better.

[6] *In Search of the Miraculous, p119*

The class itself is actually open to trying to come to a quieter, more collected state. They know this instinctively. You only need to "guide" them gently by providing the optimal conditions. Don't talk and spoil this opportunity with "instructions." This cannot come from your ego. It needs to come from a genuine wish for the higher. Sense the energy in the room and concentrate on your own efforts to be present.

The sound that comes from the class – their voices, their feet, this natural frequency of humanity is the place from which the higher will be found. Give it room and time.

Sacred Dances: The Gurdjieff Movements

CHAPTER 9

Inner Work and Energy

Many people come to the Movements class to reinforce their Inner Work for the week, and that is certainly one use for a weekly class. However, when coming to the class, one should bring one's own work and questions.

Movements classes are not for the aggrandizement of the instructor, although these days, there are many so-called instructors for whom this is all it's about. The Movements are for the class – those attending have come for an opportunity to learn something about themselves.

In Mr. Gurdjieff's day, occasionally, he would compose Movements specifically to help a particular individual. Which Movements those are and who they were for has long since been forgotten, but in working with many different Movements over time, each participant will encounter Movements which are particularly difficult for him or her and which ones he or she finds easy. This is a very big clue to one's own work on Presence.

We all have resistance. In fact, even when coming to the class, nearly everyone senses resistance. This is because there is the acknowledgment that one will be stretched, and we are all lazy, particularly mentally. All authentic Gurdjieff Movements have a difficult mental component. Sometimes, in addition, a difficult "sensational" component. This is, of course, in addition to learning the physical part, the "choreography" of the Movement. This is because Mr. Gurdjieff is showing us how to work properly with our poorly trained brains.

The mental part of the moving center can manage most of the functions of the Movement without interference from the Formatory apparatus (that which we usually call "mind").

The function of the mental center is to follow and not be distracted by the Formatory apparatus. Because of the structure of Movements, this is actually possible.

One can clearly see the Formatory apparatus operating and distracting us from learning. Alfred Etiévant used to joke about people in the class who "went out for coffee" during a Movement. Movements class is not the place to think about what is for dinner or how long something is taking. This is the moment for an increased effort of Attention.

Our unused "brains" the true intellectual center, groan with lack of use as they are challenged to follow the count, see my place in the Enneagram, visualize positions in advance, and so on and so on. This is always met with resistance, and usually, pupils try to find an "easy" way to do things, such as the attempt to describe the multiplications as 2 and 4, 1 and 5, 2 and 4,1 and 5 and 3 and 3. Mrs. Howarth pointed out that every Movement has a "catch" to make it easier to remember. That does not mean that we should use it. Those who are more physically able and those that are very intelligent see those things very quickly. But for inner development, it is necessary to work through these challenging mental exercises. For example, when one tries to visualize the rotations of the Enneagram numbers in one's head during the *Men's Enneagram Movement*, the various tempos of each center become very clear. This is an important part of Work understanding. If you just memorize which positions you need to execute in your file, you will miss this altogether. So, for your own sake, don't circumvent the required effort.

As mentioned previously, why are Movements never done by one person alone? Why is this important? Absolutely? The class represents "organic life on Earth" in a small way, but this class vibration of energy is vital to help individual inner work on oneself. We all help each other, as do the emanations emitted from the instructor and the pianist. As was said, one can see the absolutely vital necessity for the instructor to be present in themselves to be able to "see" the inner level of the class and also of particular individuals. This is not unlike "group leading." This is helping the class to realize its potential. The unfortunate truth, at this period of time, is that there are few instructors who have been taught how to do this. Not only does this need to be taught, but it takes years of work on oneself in the capacity of an instructor to be able to even adequately observe the class like this. And yet that is what Movements require.

The ability to change the level of "being" of the class is dependent on a number of factors, some of which have been mentioned in previous chapters. But most of all, it depends on the level of "being" of the Instructor. And that is why not just anyone can teach Mr. Gurdjieff's Movements. Because Movements are a physical activity, many people think naively that they are capable. And they go ahead and "teach" Movements. There are hundreds of these "teachers" around. But what are they "teaching"? There is a fundamental aspect of Movements missing.

The class enters the room with a certain level of energy. This depends on a number of things; the seasons, the temperature, the number of pupils, the light in the room, whether they know each other or not, whether it is their first or their 100th class, etc. The instructor's job is to sense this right from the beginning. This is their starting point. The seasons of the year have a lot to do with energy. I have noticed over the years that because humans are animals, in early spring, a sort of "malaise" comes over them (maybe this is why Lent was created or some of the early sacrificial times noted in *Beelzebub's Tales*). This is normal and corresponds with the call from Great Nature. But in the Movements class, the pupils often forget completely what they once knew very well, and one has to start again from the beginning.

Both in the summer and winter, one has to contend with temperature. Most Movements classes are in climate-controlled rooms, thankfully. Perspiration dripping down one's back is very distracting, and the body has an additional burden in summer of dealing with the heat as many Movements are quite active. Because this is not training the body in a physical way like, say, dancing or boxing, there is no need for this type of distraction. Classes should be held in as comfortable a temperature range as possible. This is also true of winter. Movements classes should also not be used as "warmups" or even morning wake-up classes, as I have seen done in some retreats.

Another important aspect is the room or Movements' Hall. A wooden floor, ideally a "sprung" floor with some "give" is recommended. Concrete or tiled floors have a harmful effect on the body, sending the reverberations from the feet directly up into the optic nerve of the eye. This can cause damage. Also, the spine absorbs the shock from a rhythm executed in the feet, which cannot be diffused throughout the body effectively on a hard floor. If this is all that is available, use slippers with a little padding to cushion the effect of the hard floor.

The best room for Movements is one with no windows and good air circulation. Drafts tend to blow away the emanations of the class, and windows are distracting. No mirrors either. I also would highly recommend not doing Movements outside, romantic as that may seem. We are trying to reach a very subtle energy which is very fine and difficult to sense. The outside vibrations are too coarse for this and tend to lower the Movements class to an "exercise" class; not what we are looking for.

We are looking here for something higher – another level of vibration which is very subtle and with which we are not very well acquainted. Even a single bad condition can totally destroy this effort.

As for the instructor, it is all on him/her to observe the impediments to a change of state and do something about it. The instructor should never give a class when there is something bothering the pupils – either physical or emotional, or if their mind is occupied with some problem or other. Just as the pupils do, the instructor leaves his or her ordinary self outside the door to dedicate himself and his class to a search for the higher, just as one does in sitting quietly.

Arguments over either music or time in front of the class affect the whole class. One heavily negative person will make it impossible for the class to come to any higher level.

A "bad mood" can also be provoked by the instructor in certain ways. This does not help anyone and just reduces the level of the class to pathetic. The class is not there for the instructor to "lord" over. The instructors' job is to have compassion for the Inner Work of the class and to assist it in every way possible.

There is no place for the instructor's ego in the room. This is distinct from "showing" the Movement put together to help the class have a sense of the quality of the particular Movement. That needs to be done only when necessary.

Another big pitfall in the class is sexual energy, tension and attraction. Instructors come in both genders, and there is always an interaction with the pupils that takes place. *This is something that is never spoken about and needs to be.* One of the reasons for the "dress regulations" in Movements is to remove this problem. Pupils are asked not to wear revealing clothing and to always wear supportive underwear. This comes up in every group because wearing revealing clothing is cultural for us.

Jessmin Howarth put it very well. She said, "Choose an outfit that you keep only for Movements class. It needs to not restrict the body but cover it properly and not distract from sensation. This outfit should not be worn for any other activity, so that when you put it on, it will be a preparation for the Movements class."

Over the years, things have been added to this from experience. There are to be no shirts with logos (distracting for the instructor), no tank tops, crop tops or low-cut tops. No tight jeans which stop you from bending your knees and restrict your waist. And no shirts that are so short that when you lift your arms, the belly is exposed.

All this is for two purposes; 1) to not distract the instructor and other pupils and 2) to remind the pupil that they are there for something inner, not outer.

The instructor needs to be aware of where they stand in front of the class and to make sure they circulate around the class, so as not to give any one student the impression that they are making "special" contact with them. We try never to put husbands and wives adjacent to each other. In the class, each person is there for their individual work and no coaching or criticizing of each other in class is allowed. It is important for everyone in the room that a "safe" space is created, because a lack of trust will not allow people to explore their inner world.

I tell my incipient instructors to think of the class in a "warm and caring" way. The instructor is responsible for a non-threatening class environment. Mr. Gurdjieff is not here anymore, and none of us have his Being. We do not have the right to "criticize" others.

Each person in the class has a very special inner one-on-one relationship with the instructor. This is something very peculiar to Movements and has to do with the "inner threads" that bind us together. Thus, often a pupil thinks that an instructor sees more about them than they do. Each person in the class thinks that the instructor "loves" him, and that is partly true because this is based on the "I love him who works"[7] comment made by Mr. Gurdjieff. There is a mutual understanding that comes from Inner Work, and it makes long-lasting connections.

Some Instructors "use" this connection in a sexual way. That is, of course, absolutely wrong. The conditions of the class are amplifying and sometimes create "something" that may or may not be there. This is especially a pitfall for male instructors. To have women gaze up at them with adoring and trusting eyes is a hard call. But taking

---

[7] *Views From the Real World, p251-253*

advantage of this will get you removed from instructing and probably from your Group also. Good instructors need to see the class as their "children" and treat the members of the class with respect.

The instructor's job is to "lift" the level of being of the class. This is a huge task and reminds me of the "terror of the situation." Anyone who does not fear and respect the level of this undertaking should not be giving Movements. I say a little prayer to God before each class and ask for His help. I wish for Presence both for myself and for the class. The goal for every good Movements class should be that there is at least a few moments when there is a palpable "presence" in the room. The more the better, but just as in sitting and meditating, I tell my students – "do not get up till you have sensed a different state." Make this your aim.

How does one go about this? By commanding one's own attention and the attention of those in the class.

Be present – put your whole attention on the class and "see" how they are following instructions. Where is their state? Is this too much for them? Too little? How can I give what I am teaching clearly? Did I do that?

What could help them understand the Movement better? How am I standing, moving? Is anyone confused?

Are they able to follow the sequence of the Movement and still relax? How is the tempo? And so on and so on.

Attention all the way through the class; no letting up for the instructor; observation of as much as possible while at the same time sensing oneself.

Practice the "double arrow," as mentioned before. I am "watching" myself while at the same moment observing something outside of myself. Practice, practice, practice.

Learn the ability to sense one part of the body while doing something different. And most of all, never lose sight of the fact that once you enter the Movements room, you are there to serve something higher – not to put people through their paces.

CHAPTER 10

Gradations and Planning:

Since most human beings have a short attention span and it is the goal of the instructor to help extend each person's ability to remain focused, I have found certain things very helpful.

1) Wear a watch if you cannot see a clock on any wall of the classroom. Plan for a one-hour class, and if it's a two-hour class, have a "water break" of 5 minutes in the middle.

2) In planning, divide each hour class into 15-minute segments. This is because, in 15 minutes, you can teach a segment of a Movement, and the class can absorb this material and still be alert.

   More than that, and the attention begins to wane.

   This is naturally not a hard and fast rule. It is there as a guide for you. Use your watch and see if you have gone over the 15-minute time. How is the class attention? "Help" the class. Notice if the energy of the class is weak or if they are tired, and be willing to put aside what they are doing and change to something else. Remember, the goal of the class is a change in state, not doing a Movement.

Of course, there are very advanced classes who can keep attention for the full hour, but that is very rare, and this is usually in preparation for an event where a specific Movement is being shown.

At this point, there needs to be an inner evaluation to see if the Instructor can bring the Movement and the class to a state of combined presence. Be honest.

3) Do not repeat and repeat a Movement or sections of it more than three times. After that, It is not useful for the class.

4) Divide the material ahead of time into sections based on your experience in the Movement. And obviously, never teach a Movement you have not experienced completely yourself. Look at the material and decide how you will present it. Nearly always, it will mean the structure of the Movement will come first. Be sure the structure of the Movement is clear to the class before moving to other things, like feet positions, arms, etc. Sometimes the structure is the rhythm. Make sure it is in your body when you step in front of the class.

5) When the class enters the room, there are two opinions on preparation which depend on the state of the people entering. Some people prefer to sit quietly along the perimeter of the room, while others prefer to practice. This latter was what Mrs.

Howarth preferred, but I've noticed that more and more people would rather have a break from their everyday concerns when they enter the Movements Hall.

6) After each Movement in the class is discontinued, the class should be encouraged to stand still (i.e., not twitch, rearrange clothes, for example) in order to allow the finer vibration of the Movement to penetrate and to observe the effect each Movement has on the body.

Mrs. Howarth used to recommend 11 seconds.

As has been said many times before in this text, Movements are not made for the instructor but for the students in the class.

It is vitally important for the growth of the class to give the right material at the right time.

When individuals first begin Movements, they cannot and should not do very complex Movements. This does a disservice to everyone. It spoils the impression of these very beautiful Movements when the student is ready to appreciate them, and it frustrates the beginner because they are beyond the capacity of the student.

We can divide Movements roughly into two categories for this purpose: Movements that are difficult physically to coordinate and those that require a fineness of energy and inner quiet.

Physical Difficulties

In this category are many of the early Movements, such

as *the Obligatories* and many coordination Movements. *The First Obligatory* has the demand of moving both large (legs) and small (head) body parts at an unaccustomed tempo. This is the first challenge from Mr. Gurdjieff in viewing the body in a different way. Then he moves on to the *2nd Obligatory*, which outlines the physical atmosphere around the body. In *Counting*, the *3rd Obligatory*, we see the very large Movements of the body, which are totally unusual in our daily life. Then we move into very physical positions in the *4th and 5th Obligatories*, which involve kneeling and standing and then end with the totally aerobic *6th Obligatory*. Generally, I do not start beginners with these Movements unless they are in their twenties or thirties due to the extreme physical nature of the Movements. If the students are any older than that, too much energy is expended doing the Movement, and there will be little left for a sensation of themselves in the Movement.

It also gives them the wrong impression – that Movements are all about the physical. This is probably because, in Mr. Gurdjieff's day, people did not sit around as much as they do today and generally were in better physical shape than the current population. Additionally, Gurdjieff's first students were in their 20's and 30's, and physically fit.

Other Movements that have physical difficulties are *Number 5*, with its different arms doing different things.

This study in coordination is also in *Old 21* and several other Movements that have one continuous flowing arm versus a "static" other arm.

Other sorts of coordination difficulties in Movements are with the feet versus a gesture or Movement with the arms. Since the rhythmic pattern is usually with the feet, it is the work of the Movement to tie together the movements of the upper body in synchronicity. This is very hard and takes the attention completely to the physical aspect. Not that this is a bad thing. This is refining the moving center and allowing the body to make room for another attention.

Inner Difficulties

This is where the Work comes into Movements. Movements are intended to demand Presence from the participant. We need to understand how to make a gesture with intention, not reaction. In other words, can I inhabit the position from myself rather than react to the sound from the piano? This is the main reason why Movements should never be done with recorded music. It becomes mechanical, and that is the exact opposite of Mr. Gurdjieff's ideas. I need to learn to meet the note from the music from *my* intention. This is the beginning of Inner Work. How can I take each position visualize it in advance and then assume the pose? We spent many, many years doing this exercise when I first came to Movements in the 60s when they were still very close to Mr. Gurdjieff's teaching. Intention and attention are the heart of the Movement's experience.

Movements such as *Lord Have Mercy, 40 Positions, Big*

Seven, and 6 *Positions* are some of the Movements that are executed in a tempo in which one can sense internally every position and come to each one with intention.

These Movements can be executed by beginners because they are possible since they are not too physically demanding and, at the same time, if given properly, can bring a real attention in the class.

I have, for my own use, divided the Movements I instruct into three categories which you can see on the following pages.

This is to serve as a general guide to the development of an inner structure in a group of people from the beginning of the formation of a class.

In inner development, as in everything else, there is a gradation of understanding. The class as a whole moves from coarse Movements (where everything is done very physically, even though correct, but empty,) to eventually much finer, intentionally executed Movements where it is obvious that the participants have a sense of themselves. There is an energy and presence that radiates from the class as a whole and from each of the participants. This process takes years and years and intentional Work. You can see it very clearly in the films made by Mme. de Salzmann. The contrast to this is the empty and very physical Movements seen mostly on YouTube – nearly all done by non-Gurdjieff Foundations. This is *not* Mr. Gurdjieff's Movements, although they lay claim to it.

I urge anyone who is "teaching" Movements on a regular basis to consider very carefully the pupils they are instructing and how much they understand about the Work in general. The Movements they are to learn need to come from this level of understanding, not what you would like to teach as an instructor. Remember, it is not about *your* needs, interests or likes but about what the Movements can bring to the class. And to come to this, you need to study, study, study the Movements that you know and execute them by yourself at home in the quiet of your own space or, better yet, in a class that you are participating in. Allow the Movement that you wish to give to penetrate your consciousness without comment from the head. Just do the Movement until it speaks to you. Understanding is there. One needs to be free inside to listen.

Suggestions For Movements Classes updated 2020

Please note these are NOT all the Movements there are. It is a PARTIAL list to aid in choosing appropriate movements for each class level. Movements made by Mr. Gurdjieff are in grey.

Beginners:

Grand Ensemble	Tableau (on place)
Big Seven	Lord Have Mercy Number
11 Counts	11**
Am, Om, Um, Eim (march)	La Gamme
Number 30/French 4	**2nd of March**
Dance Number 5	**Medical Gymnastics**
Forty Positions	Number 7 (rhythms–I Am)
Six Positions (Poses)	Do-Mi-Sol (original)
Slow Second Obligatory	

Actual Movements:

I Am I Wish, Always
Everywhere
Blue Red, Black Yellow
I Wish, I Am, I Can Work
Father I
Small Circles

Mr. G's Enneagram circle
**Mme. De Salzmann's Big
Positions
Basic Multiplications (feet
only)**

Good Exercises:

Advanced Physically:
(i.e., younger people or older people in good shape with
Movements experience)

Number 5
4th Pythagoras
Malista
15 Count Dervish –
(Dervish #2)
Forming Twos
July 23rd
Thirty Gestures
Multiplication #15
Multiplication #17
Multiplication #41
American #1 – the stop
Two Rhythms
Number 35/42-French
Automat
American 32-American
Automat
Old21

First Obligatory
2nd Obligatory (First
March)
Counting
Note Values
March Forward
Mazurka
Trembling Dervish
First Dervish Prayer
Vis A Vis
2nd Pythagoras
The Waltz
Sacred Goose
Oriental Dance
Women of Essentuki
I Wish to Have Being
Dervish#7
2nd Lord Have Mercy

Last Pythagoras   Ho-Ya Dervish
Lundi, Mardi   French #16 Running
Tibetan Masques   Shoemaker
American #7-I Wish To Be   Spinning
Shoulder Dervish   Rug Weaving
Polyrhythms   French #18 Body Circling

Advanced Innerly:
(Not for beginners of any kind)

Prayer in 4 Parts   Multiplication Oct 9th
Halleluia   **Father, Mother, Brother,**
L'Octave   **Sister**
LittleTibetan   The Morse Lent
Multiplication#4**   **Morse 6**
Multiplication of Three   **Circles in Displacement**
Tableaux   **Prayer of June 21* (film)**
Multiplication Oct 8th   Les Circles (seated)
The 4 Aums   **The Balancier**
Ya-Yu   **Litanies**
Prayer of October 21st   **Number 37 English**
Enneagrams 1-6   **Turning**
Multiplication #26   Adam and Eva
Multiplication #18   **Les Noms**
Do Mi Sol (film version)   Dur-Rud

Note: There are two very advanced innerly Movements which are a good introduction to sensation in Movements, Lord Have Mercy and Multiplication #4. These are starred**.

Sacred Dances: The Gurdjieff Movements

CHAPTER 11

The message... Objective Art

M r. Gurdjieff himself said "The second purpose of dances is study. Certain Movements carry a proof in them, a definite knowledge, or religious and philosophical ideas. In some of them one can even read a recipe for cooking some dish."[8]

In the many years that I have studied them, I have found this to be totally true. The Movements are a book, just like *All and Everything: Beelzebub's Tales to His Grandson*. They cover all sorts of different subjects; they are all important and relate to humanity. No wonder Mr. Gurdjieff said that the title he was most proud of was "A Teacher of Dancing."[9]

The specifics of this I will leave each reader to find out from himself or herself, but I will give you some hints as to how to find out what is encoded in the movements.

Every good Movements instructor should begin for

---

[8] *Gurdjieff's Early Talks 1914 - 1931, p 358*
[9] *All and Everything, p46 "A Teacher of Dancing."*

himself or herself a list of Principles of Movements. This is to study how to go about discovering the aim and intention of Movements.

It begins with a question. What are these Movements, and how can I understand all they have to offer? I started my list at 21 when I wanted to take the study of Movements seriously, and I urge all those who are responsible for passing them on to work on this. Please have some intention and sense of responsibility with what you are doing.

In your list, you need to have headings such as Movements with Rhythms, Dervishes, Multiplications, File Cannons, Movements with Words, Movements with Sounds, Prayers, Movements which have displacements, Movements which have different speeds, Enneagrams, and many more. Write all the Movements that you know down, and then place them in categories based on the things in them. Many Movements will be in several categories. For example, one of my favorite basic Movements is *The Grand Ensemble*.

This Movement is in my categories: Large Group Movements, Movements with Bending, Movements with a "lung" Floor Plan, Movements that Change Direction, Movements with a "Pulse" unchanging beat, and Movements in which there is a Coordination Effort with the head, arms and feet.

As you do this, examining each category, you begin to see the basis for Movements study.

In the Class

First of all, try to be empty of thoughts when you are in the class doing Movements yourself and be as present as possible for observation of whatever comes up. Secondly, do not allow your banal everyday opinions to enter your observations. By that, I mean inner chattering and commenting about irrelevancies, comments like, "He couldn't possibly be referring to….". or "Nah, can't be."

Be open. You cannot possibly be of the mental level of Mr. Gurdjieff, and he has hidden these things in plain sight, just as he did in *All and Everything*, where the knowledge is actually "between the lines" in the associations that are created and paced out by the writing style in your brain. It is the same with the Movements. The observation of what each Movement "means" comes through the associations that Mr. Gurdjieff has put there.

There are several ways you can go about researching this.

One of these is to make up an exercise – for yourself only – at home alone. Try to make a march exercise where each position of the arms or head follows naturally after the other. See if you can achieve all the directions of the body (i.e., up, down, right, left etc.) Did you provide for every possibility of posture for the body and its planes of movement?

In another exercise, try to come up with four positions that invoke a prayerful feeling. Try to make them from yourself, not copied from a Movement.

Do any of these appear in any Movements that you can think of? Where is the sensation in the body during these Movements? (Not with your head – observe the reality).

Another thing to try – choose some emotions (love, anger, self-pity, remorse). How would you go about demonstrating any of these things in a Movement without sentimentality?

Do not allow lyrical (balletic) gestures, only those that come from the joints. What did you come up with?

Make an exercise with your feet, either as a rhythm or floor-plan/displacement. If you try a foot rhythm, what is the relation of speed to your inner state?

Take a concept or a fact (i.e., the rotation of the Moon around the Earth) and make up a Movement showing that. You could also try morning, noon and night... experiment at home, alone. Not in the class.

Analysis

Mr. Gurdjieff tried several different ways to bring a "message."

Study the Movements with a cannon structure as a representative of the Law of Seven and the Octave. How many Movements does this occur in? How about the Law of Three? This is aside from and in addition to the Enneagram Movements. How many Movements are there that have the Enneagram in them? Write a list. Are they the same?

Why did Mr. Gurdjieff do the "Morse" code Movements? Did you look up the Morse code, which is not used very much anymore? What is the usefulness of this? The simplest Movement to study this in is *Adam and Eva*. There are also some prayers that use Morse Code. What are they?

There are "alphabet" Movements like Greek Letters. Why did Mr. Gurdjieff pick the Greek alphabet? Can you think of any other extremely important discipline which utilizes Greek lettering? What is the clue there?

Patterns (especially floor patterns) are also a very important clue to the message. If we examine the Enneagram (multiplication) displacements, for example, why are they elliptical?

In Chapter 44 of *Beelzebub's Tales to His Grandson* Mr. Gurdjieff describes His Self-Keepness, the Archseraph Ksheltarna, as "the Great Observer of the movements of all the concentrations of the Megalocosmos." Is it possible that some of these "displacements" of the planets are found in the Movements? Look and see if this is true.

In the Pythagoras series, what was Pythagoras famous for? Is there any evidence of this in the Movements: *2nd Pythagoras, Malista (3rd Pythagoras), 4th Pythagoras* and *the Last Pythagoras*?

In the Tibetan Series, what qualities are brought out, and how do we Westerners relate to them?

In both the Men's and Women's Movements, we have an enormous impulse to "correct" the Inner Structure of the badly warped gender structure of the modern person. This is one of Mr. Gurdjieff's greatest contributions and one he prized so much that he put these Movements at the end of the public demonstrations he gave in 1923/24. I have been teaching both Men's and Women's Movements for nearly 50 years, and I am always amazed at the understanding contained in these Movements. In order to receive anything, one needs to absolutely put aside any ideas or habits that one has from one's upbringing in this day and age. Just start from scratch, as if you were being born and being taught something new. Be open inside, and do not assume you have any of these characteristics that you observe in the Movements.

In the Men's Movements, where is the center of gravity in the body? What is Mr. Gurdjieff showing us about the use of force? From where does masculine strength come? What is the relationship between force and violence? How does one "assert" oneself in the right way? What does it mean to be a Man without quotation marks? What is the "active" force?

In the Women's Movements, where is the center of gravity? Why are there so many knee bends?

What qualities that are distinctly feminine are in these Movements that are not part of current culture? How does this relate to everyday life? How do you feel doing these Movements, and how does this relate to our current dysfunction? What does it mean to be the "passive" force?

I think that it is very necessary for everyone to have some exposure to both the Men's and Women's Movements — not as an ongoing study, but just once or twice. We all have both active and passive forces inside us, and a recognition of the sensation of each of these is part of our understanding and inner growth. What is my inner attitude towards the force of the opposite sex to our birth gender? There are also a certain number of transgender individuals that come to the Gurdjieff teaching, and many were around Mr. Gurdjieff in the 1920s. These individuals were helped in their inner understanding just as much as others, and for them, particularly, the study of Men's and Women's Movements must have been very helpful. One's gender does not affect the ability for inner understanding, which belongs to all sentient beings.

What about astronomy and astrology? Can you think of any Movements that have any of those things in them?

Look at the floor plans of Movements, and the type of displacements. Do they remind you of anything? Why are the displacements in the multiplications elliptical? Study the "word sound" OM (or AUM) and its placement in Movements. It is in many Movements. Why?

There are many hints here, but everyone needs to do the work themselves to try to "elucidate" these extraordinary Movements and experience the full value that they have hidden in them.

Sacred Dances: The Gurdjieff Movements

CHAPTER 12

The Bigger Picture – Cosmology

In the large world view, the Movements present a unique place. They are a tool for self-discovery of a kind that has been absent for many centuries.

We don't know conclusively, but it is possible that the Egyptians and the Dravidians[10] had this type of tool, but at the present time, this sort of inner exploration has been completely forgotten.

Movements are beautiful as artistic creations. The precision and the quiet grace and presence of the class inspires awe and an emotional wish for the higher. They are truly "objective art" in that they are not only beautiful but a language that can be understood via a direct emotional connection.

In the Indian tradition, we can see many beautiful ragas that are told in story form in the Bharatanatyam and other dances. But this expression is rooted in the physical and has elements of "storytelling ." Lovely to look at and

---

[10] *"Dravidian" refers to the inhabitants of the Indian subcontinent.*

classic in form, it does not influence the internal structure of the body as does Movements. From this tradition, we also have yoga. Here is a complete understanding of the body and psyche with all the elements like Movements. Of all the world's traditional "physical" forms, this is probably the closest to Gurdjieff Movements.

Part of the study of the "chakras" can also be found in Movements. Yoga is very good for the health of the body and provides a balanced psyche. However, one cannot do "downward dog" in public during the middle of the day. This is the difference with Gurdjieff Movements. Mr. Gurdjieff wanted something that could be accomplished by westerners but also something which would provide experience in sensing similar to activities during the day. How many people have done knee bends at the bus stop, trying to keep warm?

In the North American Indian tradition, we can see stories of their creation and psychic understanding in the Corn and Ghost dances. These dances, which are sometimes still performed in the Hopi Third Mesa, were once off limits to the general public because – like Movements – they contained the sacred knowledge of their ancestors. This has now changed, I believe. With pressure from the public and the onset of tourism dollars, even the sacred can be bought.

There are many examples of unity in the forms of Middle Eastern Dance, and of course, who could forget the Whirling Dervishes? This form, too, while it was created for the inner life of the participants, is not viewed very often by the public and is probably the closest thing in intention to the Gurdjieff Movements. But the Whirling Dervishes do not have the extraordinary range of the Movements as far as inner experience goes. Movements are meant to help with inner presence every day, and they have a huge range of information encoded in them. The whirling only helps you when you are whirling.

In Flamenco, the original dance of Spain brought by the Moors, there is a three-fold Work.

All real Flamenco consists of three people:- the dancer, the singer, and the guitarist. There are a set number of "forms" – songs where each has a specific beat, which is known to all three parties to the set. Then one person in the set begins with a "call" which consists of identifying the form with which to begin. From then on, all attention from all three parties is focused on each other to create and is always evolving and is always a new creation. The major focus of this art form is attention. Unfortunately, much of this has been forgotten with the rise of the ego, and we see numerous examples of guitarists who are virtuosos, dancers dancing to recorded music to show off, and the singers pretty much forgotten. The breakup of this triangle means that this is no longer Flamenco. It is just Spanish dance and music.

In the dipping and soaring of the Greek and Spanish Basque dance, there is the bird-like quality denoting freedom and a higher state. And in folk dances around the world, there is a celebration of life and sometimes of labor.

There is a category of Movements called "Work Dances." These Movements were shown last in demonstrations that were done under Mr. Gurdjieff's direction in 1923 and 1924.

Why would these Movements which appear "mundane" be the highlight of the program?

In this, we see the genius of Mr. Gurdjieff. These Work Dances are the "crossover," as it were, between inner life and outer life. He is pointing out the intentional nature that is required in daily life, which is what is necessary for real Inner Growth. Appropriate to his message. "Remember Yourself Always and Everywhere," these dances are pointing out the way to be intentional during one's daily life and work. This was, of course, much easier in a time when there were repetitive daily tasks that didn't involve electronics.

I find that classes nowadays have a hard time with these Movements, which become for them like "play-acting." This is because the vast majority of students have never spun a thread or knitted a scarf or sweater and definitely never mended shoes. I always tease them that if these exercises were called "keyboarding," everyone would get it. These Movements will probably have to be phased out at this time due to lack of relevance with the current world. Perhaps when things become simpler again, these gestures will be recognized for the gift that they are, but for the moment, we must accept that we just need to understand why these Movements are important. They are the only Movements that are not "joint-related," and they do, in fact, have a common purpose which does give the class an experience of humanity doing something together.

In the relationship of Movements to something larger and related to the universe, there is a rich field.

There are Movements which illustrate the laws of the Universe. Not only the Laws of Three and Seven but, as was pointed out before, the Enneagram.

At a vibrational level, there is something else.

We have in each class a representation of the cosmos' "energy level." The wavelengths of the energy of the class rise and fall according to Law and the conditions. It is the job of the instructor to be aware of this and act appropriately to elevate this level according to their understanding.

Within each person, there is a miniature cosmos (because we are made "in the Image of God").[11]

All the parts of the possibilities of the whole are there. And within the class, there are many gradients of inner evolution. We are all somewhere on this gradient. We were either born with some inner wish or not. My observation of it is that most people who come and continue learning from Movements are those who are already born with some of the inner atomic substance required for inner transformation. This is what is called in

_____

[11] *The Bible. Genesis 1:27, King James Version*

Ouspensky's writings "Magnetic center"[12]. This is because they recognize immediately the enormous use of these exercises and are grateful to those who bring them properly. When Movements are done regularly for many years, they do, in fact, transform the individual. I have seen many people with severe physical impairments improve significantly to the point that you would not recognize that they ever had an impairment. I have also seen the character of people change remarkably for the better.

Movements make you sleep better, relax more and remember yourself more often during your waking hours. If analyzed, they make you think about the Universe and the Laws that we are all under. But most of all, when done properly, they change your state, making it possible to see things in yourself that you could not otherwise observe. They provide a clarity of view that takes hours of meditation to come to, and they do it in seconds. This is priceless.

Thank you, Mr. Gurdjieff.

---

[12] *In Search of the Miraculous, p200*

CHAPTER 13

Movements and Other Aspects of The Work

As far as I know, Mr. Gurdjieff never intended the Movements to be done as a practice by themselves. Originally, they were part of the Workday, except for times when a demonstration was being prepared. It is notable that Movements were given mainly at the end of the afternoon on Workdays at the Prieuré, and that tradition has continued to this day during Intensive Work periods. The Work is, as has been stated previously, a three-fold system: ideas, Movements, and practical work. When this is destroyed, and emphasis is put on any one of these, eliminating the others, there is a corresponding lack of inner "help" available. To really make any headway in one's inner understanding, one needs to study all aspects of the Work together.

1) Movements in Relation to All and Everything

The stated aim of *All and Everything* is:

First Series: To destroy mercilessly, without any compromises whatsoever, in the mentation and feelings of the reader, the beliefs and views, by centuries rooted in him, about everything existing in the world.

Second Series: To acquaint the reader with the material required for a new creation and to prove the soundness and good quality of it.

Third Series: To assist the arising in the mentation and in the feelings of the reader of a veritable, nonfantastic representation not of that illusory world which he now perceives but of the world existing in reality.[13]

This is exactly what the Movements do also. First, they break down what you think you know about yourself. Then they provide a new "inner landscape." And then this changes your state so you can maintain this state and so are able to see what really "is."

Besides this, the most obvious correlations to All and Everything are in the Chapter of *Heptaparaparshinokh*, where Mr. Gurdjieff states: "Beelzebub tells how men learned and again forgot about the fundamental cosmic law of Heptaparaparshinokh."[14]

Many of the Movements have illustrations of the Law of Three and the Law of Seven.

In the case of the Law of Three, there is everything from

---

[13] *All and Everything. 1950 Edition, first page*
[14] *All and Everything. 1950 Edition Chapter XL title, p813.*

the wonderful *Do Mi Sol* to *Three Cannons*. There are many more examples to be discovered by the serious searcher. There are so many examples, in fact, that I am not going to list them here but leave it up to the reader to study that for himself or herself.

Looking at the Law of Three from an esoteric inner perspective as forces of active, passive and neutralizing, there are many Movements that have three parts, such as *Note Values*. These Movements have a segment which addresses each quality and then provides a reconciling force which is illustrated in many different ways.

The Law of Seven is most clearly illustrated in the *Big Seven*, but every Enneagram Movement does this beautifully. It can be seen both in the pattern of the Enneagram and also in the positions which show many aspects of the same thing, quite often as a rhythm, such as *Multiplication #17*.

And in *The Great Prayer* here, we see the timeline laid out in *Beelzebub's Tales*.

2) Movements related to "In Search of the Miraculous."

Please read and study the pages on the Enneagram diagram in *In Search of the Miraculous*. This is required reading for those in my Movements classes.

There are numerous Movements with references or just plain descriptions of the Enneagram in Movements. Visuals like *L'Octave* and *Multiplication #18*, as well as the rotations of the Enneagrams Numbers 1 through 6. Every multiplication (and there are many) is based on the Enneagram rotations.

3) Movements in Relation to Workdays

The Movements, as I said previously, were originally incorporated into the Workday, usually held around 4-5 pm towards the end of the day. This tradition has been continued to this day in the Gurdjieff Foundation Groups. This is in a regular "Work Weekend" or "Work Week" session where the emphasis is not on Movements but on other aspects of the Work.

This is a great combination because generally, the mornings and sometimes also the afternoon have been given over to physical work, such as gardening, painting, or construction. In recent years, the format of the Workday consists of a thoughtfully given inner "task," which the participants are given to study while executing the physical work and then carries over into the Movements class. In a well-organized Workday, this task and the Movements to be studied in the Movements class are coordinated so that the aim of inner work is available in each area. This, of course, means that the Workday should be directed by someone with a more developed Being than the participants. At least someone, "at the next lamp post in the Étoile," as Mr. Gurdjieff would have put it.[15]

From these activities come the Work Dances, spoken

---

[15] *The Étoile (star) is a large roundabout at the end of the Champs-Élysées avenue on which stands the Arc de Triomphe. See also In Search of the Miraculous, p202.*

about in the previous chapter. Originally simple actions like harvesting wheat and spinning were included in these Work Dances, and the people who came to the workdays (where they were taught spinning, weaving, and pottery) were familiar with the physical actions of these occupations. This is not true anymore, however.

Some of the Women's Movements also have occupational gestures, which, again, are unrelatable for most contemporary women.

4) Movements related to "Special Conditions."

From time to time in the Work, it is necessary to create what are called "special conditions" in which the pupils will be "stretched" in their ability to stay present.

One of these conditions is the annual Celebration of January 13th. This is not a celebration of Mr. Gurdjieff's birthday, as some have thought, but a celebration of the Eastern Orthodox New Year, which Mr. Gurdjieff wished. Under these conditions, the students prepare food, decorations, and a presentation – sometimes of Movements. There is always opportunity for Inner Work and the study of intention. Currently, the biggest privilege is to prepare for the big event – rather than attending it.

Another "special condition" is a Movements Demonstration." This can be public (rarely) or just within the group.

The idea here is not to "show off" the Movements facility of students, but to bring an additional challenge to attention and presence for those working in the class.

Sacred Dances: The Gurdjieff Movements

CHAPTER 14

Children's Movements

Having taught children Movements for many years, let me be very clear – "Movements" as brought by Mr. Gurdjieff are *not* for children. They were composed for the adult body. Children *do not need* Movements. Children's attention is better than adults, and their Moving Centers have not yet acquired the habitual postures and gestures that are ingrained in the adult.

That being said, adults always feel that they wish to give their children the best, and that goes for exposing them to Movements. If this is the case, there is a program of sorts that I have developed with help from Jose de Salzmann, Peggy Flinsch and Mme. Natalie Etiévant.

To begin, one needs to understand the reason and composition behind Movements. That means studying them. I tell my students to begin with a blank sheet of paper. On it, write the names (recognizable to you) of all the Movements that you know well. Then examine each of them and try to put them into categories. You will see that for some of them, this is very easy, and for some not. Many will be in multiple categories.

For example, an easy category would be **Movements with rhythms, not just tempo.** Into this category falls *Number 38/45.* Let's look at that for a moment. This Movement also falls into the category of "*Canons*" since the format of the Movement is 1 - 6 and then backwards 6 -1. And then rotating 2, 3, 4, 5, 6, 1 and backwards 1, 6, 5, 4, 3, 2, etc. It is also in the category of "*Big Positions*" because, on each rhythm, you do one large position, the same one on each count.

After a while working at this task, you will see that there are several categories for each Movement. These "categories" will become your Principles of Movements understanding. Examine each category carefully. You will see that often Mr. Gurdjieff has made seven examples of a principle during the Movement. (*i.e., Big Seven*) And sometimes, there are 3, which will be repeated again and again during the Movement. (*i.e., Do Mi Sol*).

Utilizing these principles allows you to compose material suitable for children.

Take, for example, the category "**Big Positions**" above. I made up a Movement based on this principle with the cartoon characters familiar to the age group of the class. The canon was File 1 – Superman, File 2 – Batman, File 3 – Green Lantern, File 4 - Wonder Woman, File 5 – The Flash and File 6 – Aquaman.

The children were then asked to make up their own

positions to illustrate these characters, which they were all familiar with. This serves the dual purpose of creativity for each of them, plus memory of what the others choose (similar to Mr. Gurdjieff's original exercise of Copying.) You could do this with any set of characters that the children were familiar with. – The cast of Sponge Bob, the cast of Sesame Street, and the cast of Masters of the Universe. Then after they made up their characters, you have them take the positions in canon (one after the other) just like an adult Movement. But this is completely subjective, not imposing an imitation of anything they don't understand, and the principle of this exercise is quite complete. This exercise would have the principles: Big Positions, Canons, Retain from Memory While Doing Something Else, (also called Visualization), Moving on the First Note of the Beat, and could include either Tempo or Rhythm.

If you go over your list of Principles or categories, there will be ample material to come up with a very entertaining, and useful class for any age children.

Stay absolutely away from Prayers (not that children don't pray but try not to put ideas into their heads – leave this open for their own discovery). You will find that children don't take well to slow Movements or exercises unless it is speeding up and then slowing down!!

One of the most enjoyable for children was a "Machine Group" exercise that I made up. A Machine Group is a Movement where every file and every row does something different, and they do it either all together or one at a time. Kids *love* this. It's cool having your turn as part of the "machine." This can look quite robotic but is actually a very good work on the attention. And being part of something is what everyone wishes for.

Another big hit with the children was the Multiplication of Colors. (Absolutely *no* numbers). In this exercise, each row was assigned the color of the sashes in the adult class. Only six files. Using a colored board with the corresponding post-It notes, they were told which was the "rest position" (which was, in fact, the rainbow) and then when they first displaced, they took the color sequence of the 1st Multiplication (without knowing it was that). For example: Rest "rainbow" position …

File 1	File 2	File 3	File 4	File 5	File 6
Red	Orange	Yellow	Green	Blue	Purple

(1st Multiplication – called something else – not multiplication – maybe "First time Forward")

File 1	File 2	File 3	File 4	File 5	File 6
Yellow	Green	Blue	Purple	Orange	Red

… and return to "rainbow" position. Don't mention any numbers of any kind, and make the displacements fun by being fast and returning to the "rainbow" position (rest) quickly.

In exploring the very large vocabulary of Movements, you will no doubt come to the question of the meaning of the "positions." We know that Mr. Gurdjieff composed these with a specific intention to bring about a certain state. With children, we cannot do that because we do not understand enough about children's psyche and shouldn't mess with it. One of the most interesting exercises I came to was to ask children to "make" something with their bodies. For example, I turned around and gave them my back, and I told them to make a "crown," and I would give them till the count of 20 to do it. Imagine my surprise when they held hands and lifted them up in a circle to make the "points" of the crown. They jiggled their feet for the "jewels." Sometimes, each child would make a "crown" on the top of each one's head. There are things you can ask for that promote creativity and, at the same time, should not be too esoteric. Try to concentrate on things that are in their worldview. Can be adjectives, too, like "strong" or "skinny."

To discover more about this kind of exercise, spend some time alone and try to ask yourself how you would represent certain words and then take those positions.

For example:

A good one is "Wish." What position of the body illustrates this? How about "I"? These are not for children, only for your own understanding.

These personal experiments can open many doors to the understanding of the core principles that make up Mr. Gurdjieff's Movements. Try to be honest in yourself.

As far as real "Gurdjieff Movements," there are only a very few that are appropriate for children. They are the *Mazurka (6th Obligatory)* and *Counting (3rd Obligatory)*, *Canon French #30* and *Forming Twos*. And that's it.

Make your classes full of fun exercises based on real Gurdjieff Principles. Be prepared because, in a class of 30-40 minutes, one must have about 14 different exercises available and the ability to move quickly from one to the next.

"*Stop and Go*" is one of my kid's favorites. As is "*Statues*," which Mr. Gurdjieff himself used to play with kids on the lawn of the Prieuré.[16]

---

[16] *Told to me by both Mme. de Salzmann and also by Peggy Flinsch*

CHAPTER 15

Movements and The Work Today

Well, as predicted by Mr. Gurdjieff, the wonderful system that he brought has almost disappeared under the relentless "wiseacring" of those who know nothing but wish to prop up their egos. It is unfortunate, but probably law conformable, that there is such a "pouring from the empty into the void" at present.

Much of this is the result of exactly what Mr. Gurdjieff identified – a lack of an understanding of law as it applies to humanity. On the scale of the Ray of Creation expressed so well in Ouspensky's *In Search of the Miraculous*, civilization is descending with rapidity into chaos.[17]

I often think of *Plato's Republic* as a wonderful description of the current climate. We have no Philosopher King, no King Solomon, so true chaos reigns. It seems that as every year passes we get further and further from understanding that organic life on earth has

---

[17] *In Search of the Miraculous –Ray of Creation. p169*

a place and needs to obey the higher laws that govern this planet, or nothing works.

The basic concept of Trinity, the Law of Three, and the position of the Father in the household, which is the mundane correlation of the higher law on earth, has diminished to such a state that men are finding it very difficult to find their place. As a result, women have been taking the place traditionally assigned to men. This is mainly in Western cultures but it is happening now in the East as well. We can see a general change overall in the shift from male-dominated culture to female-dominated culture. We also know that in the past, there have been many matrilineal societies. We know that from the "Mother Goddess" figurines found from the Neolithic, such as the Venus of Willendorf.

But at the present time, we are experiencing this shift in which the formerly Active (Male) and Passive (Female) roles are reversing (which, by the way, is also described in *All and Everything, Chapter 50* on *Heptaparaparshinokh*). The female role is becoming active, and the male role is becoming passive. Because of this, the Work and especially Movements that are not structured this way are becoming difficult to instruct. Most of the women and men that I have taught struggle with the basic concepts of femininity and masculinity that are presented in the Movements. This is part of the reason why certain individuals have treated the Movements as "dance" because this is the only way that they can understand them.

It is also interesting to note that Mme. de Salzmann, being a woman, softened Movements that were more direct when given by Mr. Gurdjieff. As someone who learned from a man very close to Mr. Gurdjieff (Alfred Etiévant), I can see a specific difference in the quality of the Movements presented by Mme. de Salzmann in the films produced by her. This is not to say that there is anything wrong with that, but it is interesting to observe. Of course, the quality would be different. And I'm sure Mr. Gurdjieff expected it to be. He chose Mme. and had the greatest respect for her understanding. Mme. de Salzmann can only bring what is real for her, and she tried her best to bring what is relevant for the times in which we live. Otherwise, Movements would not be "in the moment," and that is the most important part of the Work.

So, in general, I regard the inner work in both Men's and Women's Movements as an opportunity which we don't have in life now. Each gender can experience inside themselves either their affinity for a particular gesture or movement or an intense dislike. This is useful in the search for "Who I Am." I see where I have no relation inside myself. Or where I have an unexpected one with the gender that I identify with.

As far as the meditation aspect of the Work goes, there are now so many "experts" in this field that it is up to the meditator to find the path that suits him/her. The Work "sittings" are just one of the ways. It is important to note that actual "sittings," which we have now, were not given that way by Mr. Gurdjieff. This current trend toward meditation was brought by Mme. de Salzmann and William Segal after a visit to Dr. Suzuki. Mr. Gurdjieff did give many pointers for sensation and self-observation, which can be seen in *Views From the Real World*,[18] and also in *Paris Meetings 1943*[19] but it is different from the ritualized sitting which we have now. Meditation was *never* the center point of the Work, which people have been led to believe.

The Workdays are now virtually obsolete. For many years the emphasis was on crafts such as weaving, spinning, pottery, glass blowing, and writing which correlated well with the "hippie" ideals of communal living back to the land in the commune era. This has given way at the present time to an emphasis in life on consumerism.

Local handmade goods are almost disappearing here in America with the import/export from various nations and the lack of interest in learning a craft. We still have a few holdovers in the Gurdjieff Foundations of people with such expertise, but it is increasingly rare. So Workdays at the present time usually focus on food preparation and gardening or construction rather than crafts. The general work of the day is interrupted by several short sessions of meditation and then group discussion, which makes the whole Workday much more monastic than previously. This only increases the tendency for "wiseacring" instead

---

[18] *Views from the Real World, Prieuré Jan 20th, 1923 p236-243.*
[19] *Paris Meetings 1943,Dolmen Meadows Editions 2017*

of real quality observations.

Mr. Gurdjieff himself predicted that his Work would not last beyond the "fourth generation" after him, and he was, as usual, right.

Sacred Dances: The Gurdjieff Movements

How I became a Movements Instructor

When I was around eight years old, my very wise mother decided to send my younger sister, Fiona, and me to ballet school. I loved it. I loved moving, and I loved the music.

So my young life and that of my sister became filled with three days a week of torture at the barre. However, I could see that this built both stamina and muscle as I was a rather skinny kid. It also was a wonderful confidence builder and brought some understanding of sensation, which I did not know how to articulate at the time, about the spine and "pulling yourself up out of your hips," which stood me in great stead later.

Beside loving the music, I also appreciated my life in ballet for the impressions it gave me.

I will never forget my Grade One Cicchetti exam. Here I was – this small skinny waif of a child – standing in this vast cavernous, cold room (the now St. Lawrence Hall). The examiners smiled kindly and said – "Just dance for us – anything you want." I wondered how could anyone so tiny as I make an impact in this huge, huge space. I felt my size and shape and the proportions of the room so clearly. This was the start of my impression of a body taking up space which would come again as I grew older.

So I continued my three-times-a-week ballet lessons until the age of 13, when something remarkable happened. My parents, Trevor and Mary Elizabeth (Elsa) Denzey, had brought their two girls from England so that my father could go to MIT on a scholarship from General Electric.

My parents met some friends at GE – Paul and Sheila Bura, and together with the Buras, they became part of the first Toronto Gurdjieff Group with Margot and Ernest Dustan, Eve Plewes, Hal Boacher, Madeline Rose, and Joe and Dolores Victor. At this time, the Toronto Gurdjieff Group – which had been the province of Mme. de Hartmann, was given by Mme. de Salzmann to Mrs. Louise Welch, who was a pupil of Orage, to oversee. This was around 1955. There were a couple of times when we were left alone in the parking lot of the then Center Stage building (which is where The Hudsons Bay Company is now in central Toronto). This was perfectly safe in those days. You couldn't do it now. And we would amuse ourselves for the hour – often looking in the window to see what kind of "dancing" our parents were doing.

Then one day, my mother bought us two new white

suitcases, and she started to pack them with clothes for each of us. I asked what she was doing, and she said, "You're going to camp". I asked, "What kind of camp? Why aren't you packing any swimsuits? Oh, she said, somewhat flustered – I'll put one in". I pointed out that I hated day camp. She said that I would probably like this one, it was not day camp but more like a summer boarding school, and so my sister Fiona and I were sent off to JFK Airport by ourselves as "Unaccompanied Minors" in charge of the airlines to meet someone whose name we didn't know in New York. It was not the first time we had flown or the first time we had been in New York, so we did have some idea of what to expect.

However, when we disembarked from the plane at JFK, there was no one there to meet us, so I, as the big sister, tried to be responsible, and I called my mother on the phone to say "there was no one here." She assured me that someone was coming and to wait patiently. And we did - for two hours. Imagine two little girls, then 10 and 13, alone in NYC dressed in pink dresses and black patent leather shoes!

Now I realize that it was Friday evening, and the plane arrived at rush hour. JFK is at the very farthest reaches of New York proper, and the gentleman who came to pick us up had never been to JFK and was from New Jersey. And so, he finally arrived and whisked us into a car to drive us to a strange location that we weren't told about. After an hour or two in the car, he stopped the car at a diner and asked us if we would like some dinner.

I thought this an excellent idea since we hadn't eaten since we left Toronto. In my childish way, I thought, "At least if I'm going to die or be kidnapped, I won't be hungry!"

After eating, it was back into the car for another hour-long ride into the blackness. I truly thought we might fall off the end of the Earth. There was not a light anywhere. I resigned myself to my fate, thinking that we could possibly die.

Then finally, the car stopped in front of a farmhouse, and there on the front porch, to my intense relief, was Larry Rosenthal – my mother's good friend and fellow pianist who had often stayed with us at our home in Oakville.

The next day, all the children, aged from 9 to 12 (about 30 of us) from all over the world, had breakfast and were given our "assignments" for the day. Certainly, there was no mention of swimming, and it all sounded like work to me. I did not have a good opinion of this "summer camp". Nevertheless, I clambered into the beat-up "woodie" station wagon up to the "Main House." To say it was impressive would be an understatement. This was the mansion Franklin Farms, Mendham, New Jersey, where Madame Ouspensky was then living. But I didn't know that at the time.

In the afternoon, Peggy Flinsch, who was in charge of the children, came over and told me that the Movements class was starting, and I was to come into the salon. I emphatically refused, stating that I was not going to do those "things." I knew that somehow they were the center of the "religion" or "teaching" or whatever it was that my parents were interested in, and I had no intention of anyone dragging me into it without my volition. Peggy, being the shrewd person that she was, responded, "Well, Nella, you look like a fair person to me. Would you agree to coming to three Movements classes? Then if you really don't like it – you don't have to come again". I agreed.

But what I was not prepared for was what happened in the first class. I was placed at the back of a class of about 30 children of all different sizes, and with my years of ballet training, I was astonished that I could not do the exercises that were given as fast as children much younger than me. They had so much better attention than I did. I was shocked. Sitting at the front of the room was a white-haired lady (who only later would I learn was Mme. de Salzmann herself) and Jim Nott (Stanley Nott's son). At the piano in this gorgeous room with French windows was Larry Rosenthal and my mother's friend Millie Morganstern.

I tried my best to pay attention and "get" the exercises. Then something remarkable happened. I know that this seems impossible – but I am giving you the absolute truth. At the top of my head, I looked up and saw a beam of light – quite wide and very bright.

In the beam, on either side, were people whom I instantly knew were souls from another time, and they were smiling and waving to me! They were all very happy to see me, and they were welcoming me into a place apparently meant for me, and they appeared to be waiting for me. I knew that this was right. Absolutely right. And this was the place that I was destined for. And so I am still here, teaching Movements to others 'til this day.

I later wrote a poem about this experience, and I put it

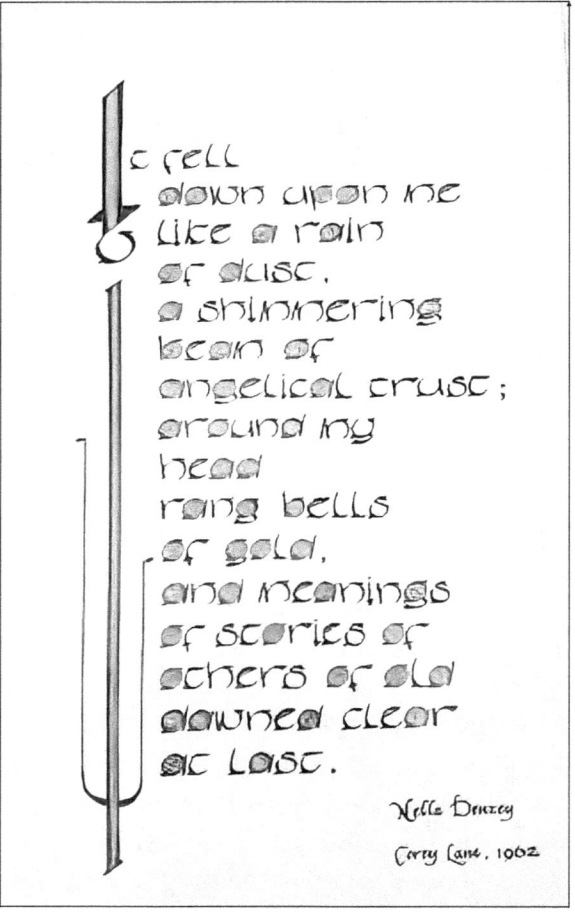

It fell
down upon me
like a rain
of dust,
a shimmering
beam of
angelical trust;
around my
head
rang bells
of gold,
and meanings
of stories of
others of old
dawned clear
at last.

Nelle Denzey

Carey Lane, 1962

in a copy of *Meetings With Remarkable Men* that we had at home, which I happened to be reading. I really didn't want anyone to see it. My father found it a few months later in the book and calligraphed it in a script based on the Enneagram. Then he sent a copy to Mme. de Salzmann. Mme. must have been very amused when she got it. Now I know that she was expecting it.

After that event, when Fiona and I returned home, we had regular Movements classes for children with some others who were the children of other people in the Toronto group. Our main teacher was Alfred Etiévant, who was a wonderful teacher. Quick as a whip, solid and strong, he delighted in playing rhythmic games with us. I used to make him laugh since he would give me up to seven different rhythms to remember, and I could get them all right! It was a friendly competition between us. Alfred said to my mother that we were both "future Movements teachers." And we certainly proved him right. I learned many Movements from Alfred and was very sad when he died of cancer and hepatitis when I was 18. He was only 37. I will remember him always with great affection and appreciation for all that he did for me. He even talked my father into giving me much-needed braces for my teeth.

After the adult Movements classes, the group sat against the walls of the Movement's Hall and listened to a chapter of *Beelzebub's Tales to his Grandson*.

In between Alfred's visits, we had the luxury of the wonderful Olga Adie. Trained in the Paris group, Olga

was Burmese and married to George and Helen Adie's son Thomas. My parents became very good friends with the Adies, and we spent many a weekend with them at their chinchilla farm in Uxbridge, where the first summer intensive period for the newly formed Gurdjieff Foundation of Toronto was held.

I admired Olga's teaching of the Movement's class. She instructed Movements very well, and I admired her many talents. She even gave me her dress (above) which I wore till it fell apart.

Shortly after Alfred's death, I went to New York for the opening of a new location for the Gurdjieff Foundation of New York. It was called Armonk, after the town where this former nunnery was purchased. There were 350 people at the first "10-day" period. The group decided for some reason to have a "July 4th Barbecue celebration". I was thrilled because July 4th was my birthday. You can imagine how I felt when the whole throng sang me "Happy Birthday." I was 21. And then and there, I made a pledge which I have kept to this day.

"I pledge to be a responsible three-brained being in every respect, to help with the sorrow of his Endlessness. To be responsible for myself both outerly and innerly and help as many others as I can to do the same."

And after that event, I met my husband and moved to New York so that I could be closer to Mme. de Salzmann and the Work that I loved.

www.ingramcontent.com/pod-product-compliance
Lightning Source LLC
Chambersburg PA
CBHW071401120626
46546CB00002B/765